# Inequality and the
# Labyrinths of Democracy

# Inequality and the Labyrinths of Democracy

Göran Therborn

**VERSO**

London • New York

First published by Verso 2020
© Göran Therborn 2020

An earlier version of Chapter 2 appeared in *New Left Review* I/103, May–
June 1977. An earlier version of Chapter 3 appeared in Rolf Torstendahl
(ed.), *State Theory and State History*, London: Sage 1992.

1 3 5 7 9 10 8 6 4 2

**Verso**
UK: 6 Meard Street, London W1F 0EG
US: 20 Jay Street, Suite 1010, Brooklyn, NY 11201
versobooks.com

Verso is the imprint of New Left Books

ISBN-13: 978-1-78873-899-6
ISBN-13: 978-1-78873-898-9 (HBK)
ISBN-13: 978-1-78873-900-9 (UK EBK)
ISBN-13: 978-1-78873-901-6 (US EBK)

**British Library Cataloguing in Publication Data**
A catalogue record for this book is available from the British Library

**Library of Congress Cataloging-in-Publication Data**
A catalog record for this book is available from the Library of Congress

Typeset in Sabon by MJ & N Gavan, Truro, Cornwall
Printed and bound by CPI Group (UK) Ltd, Croydon CR0 4YY

# Contents

CONTENTS

# List of Tables

# Preface

Two aims have directed this book, firstly to contribute to an understanding of capitalist democracy – its rise and contemporary malfunctioning – and secondly to contribute to the 'egalitarian Enlightenment', a multidisciplinary scholarly current spearheaded by Thomas Piketty and a phalanx of prominent economists, only now becoming fully visible as a major intellectual force.[1]

Born and raised in a democratic country, and an anti-imperialist and anti-capitalist since my teens, I have always been intrigued by the workings of actually existing democracies, and how they have sponsored and often perpetrated discrimination, inequality, oppression, violence and injustice. These concerns have drawn me to scholarship – historical and contemporary – and to political demonstrations.

Today, problems of democracy and inequality have acquired a new urgency. Across Natoland and its environs, crisis is the defining feature of our politics, and inequality a central concern of academic economists as well as a public worry of the high bourgeoisie, from the Davos World Economic Forum to the *Financial Times*.

For egalitarian democrats these are difficult but also fascinating times, full of contradictory tendencies and urgent socio-ecological issues. We seem caught in a quagmire, with no obvious way out. The dilapidated and perverted democracy we have is unlikely to be completely obliterated. Although a turn to a popular social democracy is scarcely on the horizon, it is less improbable than a collapse into Fascism. An egalitarian world remains a long way off, but inequality between countries is falling slightly, and within a number of countries its growth has at least decelerated. Scenes of extreme poverty amidst plenty are less common than before. We are standing at the threshold of a new anti-egalitarian onslaught from automation and machine learning, but within the academy we are also witnessing a surge of radical intellectual activity. No occasion for despair or resignation, therefore, but rather for moral integrity and for sober long-term reflection, for remembering the history of democratic struggles, for reclaiming that popular legacy, and for looking into the future through the contradictions of the present.

This volume comprises three essays on the questions of democracy and inequality, from different periods. The earliest, 'The Rule of Capital and the Rise of Democracy', appeared in *New Left Review* in the summer of 1977, almost half a century ago, when the horizon looked red.[2] It is an empirical exploration, written in the midst of a Marxist theoretical trilogy,[3] of how developed capitalism had come to be governed by democratic politics – a state of affairs that conservative, liberal and socialist opinion in the nineteenth century had all agreed was completely untenable. The essay had a sequel, 'The Travail of Latin American Democracy', published in the same journal two years later. It is not re-printed here, because so much has happened to democracy in Latin America since that time that a quite substantial update would have been necessary.[4]

This collection therefore jumps ahead in time to 'The Right to Vote and the Four World Routes to/through Modernity', an essay dating from the doldrums of progressive politics in the early nineties. It was written for an international, interdisciplinary study, *State Theory and State History* (1992), edited by Rolf Torstendahl. It is a succinct global history of elective politics, conveying, I think, something of the joy of scholarly source-digging.

These two essays are reprinted here with only minor revisions. Among the omissions are short discussions of the research situation at the time, and no update in that respect has been added. While scholarship on democracy has certainly advanced and deepened since the seventies, I don't think it has falsified my two main theses.

Both essays claim historical discoveries. The first identified how liberal democracy arose from the contingent play of the contradictions of capitalism, and was sustained by the expansion and elasticity of the latter. Research for the second uncovered four major and enduring pathways to modernity and the nation-state, and thus to contemporary elective politics: an auto-centred but world-exploiting European pathway; the secession of the New World settler states; the emancipation of the Colonial Zone; and the exceptional survivors of European conquests, the countries of Reactive Modernization, led by Japan. This global matrix of modern social development I have expanded and deployed in several later works, above all in *The World* (2011) and *Cities of Power* (2017).

From my Latin American research, the main surprise was the discovery of the importance of a stable state order for democracy as well as for levels of inequality. The protracted (civil) wars of independence and national power in Hispanic America and in Haiti left a legacy not only of devastation, but also of militarized and deeply fractured societies and polities, inhibiting continuous political as well as social and economic development. Lack of a stable state order has weighed differently on Latin American countries, but its effects are still visible. Between 1950 and 1990, there were forty-four regime changes to and from democracy in Latin America, as compared to seventeen in Sub-Saharan Africa and eleven in Southeast Asia, and the reformist policies embarked upon in the first decade of this century have been abruptly and brutally discontinued in several countries.[5]

The opening essay for this collection, 'Dysfunctional

Democracies', was written specially for it, in the autumn and winter of 2019–20, in the context of the more critical political ambience of the post-2008 period. It looks back on the social forces fighting for democracy – their demands, hopes and dreams – presenting them as a legacy to be reclaimed by people today in their confrontations with the current political caste. The essay follows up the development over time of the relations between capital and democracy, and surveys the possibilities for future change – which do exist, out of a tangle of contradictions, conflicts, and social and intellectual movements. However, social transformation will most likely require a *disruptive democracy*, of disruptive social movements, a process different from both the main twentieth-century paradigms of socio-political change: the gradual accumulation of organizational and electoral force, and violent revolution.

On the threshold of a new decade, there are two reasons for optimism. One is the new egalitarian Enlightenment in the social sciences, led by the Paris School of Economics. The political and economic consequences of the eighteenth-century Enlightenment were varied and convoluted. We should not expect many straightforward effects from that of our time. Nevertheless, the classical Enlightenment was culturally epochal and inspired revolutions in Europe and the Americas.

The other beacon in the contemporary political darkness is the climate movement, *the* generational political experience for youth today, comparable to the movements against colonial wars, racism and patriarchy that marked my generation. While climate-change awareness has spread among liberal elites, the kind of profound socio-economic transformation which climate scientists and the young climate activists think is necessary to avoid a planetary disaster can only be brought about by an egalitarian world of peaceful coexistence and cooperation, where people can trust that everybody contributes. The Battle for the Planet will require a world of cohesion similar to that which defeated Fascism in the Second World War. This may sound a radical utopia, but it highlights the intrinsic affinity and mutual dependence of egalitarianism and planetary environmentalism.

Göran Therborn
Ljungbyholm, Sweden

*Postscript.* The manuscript of this book was handed in just before the outbreak of the COVID-19 pandemic. As I write this note, in late April 2020, the pandemic is still raging, and it remains unclear whether the novel coronavirus will ultimately hit those continents off the main thoroughfares of globalization – South Asia, Africa, and Latin America – as extensively and possibly even more devastatingly than it has East Asia, Western Europe, and North America. However, it is already obvious that the pandemic has caused the largest social disruption since World War II. Will the longer-term impact of COVID-19 be of a similar scale to 1939–45? No answers are meaningful yet. Nevertheless, the crucial relevance of the pandemic's outcome to this book's concerns, namely social justice and popular power, may legitimate a sketch, however provisional, of lessons, options, and scenarios. This can be found in the conclusion to Chapter 1.

A respected voice of the cosmopolitan bourgeoise, the Editorial Board of the *Financial Times* (3 April 2020), recalls the 1940s dream of a better world to come. 'To demand collective sacrifice you must offer a social contract that benefits everyone', it acknowledges.

Radical reforms – reversing the prevailing policy direction of the last four decades – will need to be put on the table. Governments will have to accept a more active role in the economy. They must see public services as investments rather than liabilities, and look for ways to make labour markets less insecure. Redistribution will again be on the agenda ... Policies until recently considered eccentric, such as basic income and wealth taxes, will have to be in the mix.

The aftermath of World War II gave us the UN, the agenda of human rights, and the welfare state – both in Britain, with its now iconic NHS, and in several other countries. Many humane dreams foundered on the rocks of reshuffled big power geopolitics. However, 1945 should perhaps above all be remembered as the launch pad for 30 to 40 years of the most profound equalization processes in human history, dismantling institutional colonialism, defying racism and patriarchy, raising life expectancy, and reducing privileges of income and wealth.

# 1

## Dysfunctional Democracies

Democracy emerged out of mass struggle against inequality, privilege and social injustice. But after a short period in which genuine progress was made, roughly between 1945 and 1980 (and in South America, in the first twelve to fifteen years of the present century) the share of life's possibilities allocated to the descendants of the historical champions of democracy – the popular classes – has been shrinking. Why is this happening, and can the trend be reversed?

Inequality has increased, but not because ordinary people do not care about it. Inequality is in fact a common and persistent concern. Between 1987 and 2009 the International Social Survey programme asked people across the world what they thought of income differences in their country. On average, 79 per cent responded that they were too large.[1] Similarly, a 2014 survey of forty-four countries by the American Pew Research Center found that inequality was considered a 'big problem' by

Table 1. 'Inequality Is a Big Problem': Median Percentages of World Regions

|  | Big problem | Very big problem |
|---|---|---|
| Africa | 93 | 74 |
| Europe* | 91 | 60 |
| Latin America | 82 | 60 |
| Asia | 82 | 43 |
| US | 78 | 46 |
| Middle East | 74 | 57 |

* East and West, but excluding Russia and Ukraine.

Source: American Pew Research Center, 8 November 2014.

huge majorities.[2] It is, apparently, preoccupying the global elite as well. According to a survey by the World Economic Forum, 'deepening economic inequality' was the number one concern of its Global Agenda Council members.[3]

Another Pew survey in 2018 found evidence of widespread political dissatisfaction. On average, 51 per cent of respondents across twenty-seven countries were unhappy with how their democracy was functioning. Popular anger was directed at politicians and the electoral process. Sixty per cent of respondents believed that 'no matter who wins an election, things do not change very much'. The same proportion rejected the proposition that 'elected officials care what ordinary people think'. In the US, seven out of ten respondents were convinced that 'most politicians are corrupt'. In Greece and South Africa, the ratios were even higher.[4]

Discontent with democracy is clearly correlated with perceptions of the economic situation and of economic opportunity. According to Pew:

> In 24 of 27 countries surveyed, people who say the national economy is in bad shape are more likely than those who say it is in good shape to be dissatisfied with the way democracy is working. In the other three countries surveyed, so few people say the economy is good that this relationship cannot be analyzed ... In 26 of 27 nations, those who believe their country is one in which most people cannot improve their standard of living are more likely to be dissatisfied with the way democracy is working.[5]

In this way, discontent with actually existing democracy is associated with economic inequality – although people, of course, also have other reasons to be frustrated.

## I. The Labyrinthine History of Democracy

Democracy means rule of the people, a simple, literal definition, which should never be lost sight of through the intricacies of political science or the mists of liberal ideology. Aristotle put it very well about 2,300 years ago: 'A democracy exists whenever those who are free and not well-off, being in the majority, are in control of government.'[6] It might well be objected that by this definition there is currently hardly any specimen in existence. But that is hardly the fault of Aristotle.

The development of what today is nevertheless called democracy has been a labyrinthine process with many complicated twists and unexpected dead-ends. The subsequent essays in this volume are contributions to that historiography. Here, I will draw out the contrast between the democracy that popular forces fought for (at the risk, and sometimes at the cost, of their lives) and the dysfunctional democracies we have ended up with today.

### Modern beginnings

Popular rule was put on the modern political agenda by radical Jacobins aligned with the Parisian populace, the *sans-culottes*, in the French Revolution. Robespierre was the main spokesman for universal (male) suffrage, based not just on the equality of man but also on the social obligation of the state to provide 'subsistence to all its members' and to put education 'within reach of all citizens'.[7] The 'section' assemblies of the *sans-culottes* combined universal male suffrage with the principle of revocative popular representatives under popular scrutiny and control, and with broader social demands for equality of *jouissances*, the pleasures, the good things of life.[8]

The French Revolution ended in self-destructive Terror, capitalist corruption, the Napoleonic Empire, and a half-blown

Restoration of the *ancien régime*. But its democratic legacy soon surfaced. Alphonse de Lamartine, the famous poet and future leader of the Second Republic, published a brochure in 1832 advocating universal suffrage, as well as free public education, public social assistance and the abolition of slavery.[9] In the bourgeois 'reform banquets' preceding the 1848 revolution, toasts were raised to universal suffrage and admiration expressed for the radical leaders of the Revolution – Danton, Robespierre, Saint-Just.[10]

By a decree of 5 March 1848, the provisional government of the February Revolution installed general male suffrage, swelling the number of voters from 250,000 to 9 million.[11] The ensuing election, called for Easter Sunday, was the first mass democratic poll in world history, fully and freely competitive and including all political currents, with their vastly different resources. After mass, voters trooped off in alphabetical order to the centre of the canton, often hours away, led by the local priest and the mayor. Turnout was 84 per cent, but higher in the countryside than in the cities – radical Paris in particular. The intelligent Right, which had pushed for rapid elections, had calculated correctly. In a still predominantly rural France, not a single peasant was elected, and only a few workers. Conservative republicans, including camouflaged monarchists, were in a modest majority among the 880 elected deputies, while clear monarchists outnumbered radical republicans.[12]

This lesson in how to manage the people within a democratic process was taken up by leading conservative politicians in the major European states, first by Louis Napoleon Bonaparte who turned the Second Republic into a personal empire, and later by Disraeli and Bismarck, although popular pressure ultimately overtook the schemes of these gentlemen, issuing into liberal democratic government: in France after the military defeat and the Paris Commune of 1871, in Germany after the military defeat and November Revolution of 1918, and in undefeated Britain by instalments.

Was the United States another democratic trailblazer? Jill Lepore's recent history, *These Truths*, argues that by the 1830s, the US had developed into 'the first largescale popular democracy in the history of the world'.[13] Although it is true that something largescale and popular had developed in the US by this point, it fell short of Lepore's billing. The aim of the American War of Independence had not been democracy at all, but a 'republic'. According to James Madison the difference between democracy and a republic was representation, 'the delegation of government to a small number of citizens elected by the rest'. A republic could govern a large state, whereas (direct) democracies were confined to smaller ones. In Madison's eyes a republic also had another advantage, perhaps even more important: it could rein in the 'ruling passions or interests' of the majority.[14]

Racism is constitutive of all settler polities, to legitimate the appropriation of land belonging to other peoples. The US offers no exception to the rule. One illuminating piece of evidence is a letter by George Washington labelling the British governor of Virginia, Lord Dunmore, an 'Arch Traitor to the Rights of Humanity' who needed to be 'instantly crushed'.[15] Dunmore's crime had been to proclaim that slaves and indentured servants who enrolled with the British would be emancipated. Washington was the owner of hundreds of slaves.[16] 'The decades after 1815 witnessed a deepening commitment to excluding all but free whites from membership in the American body politic', observes Robert Parkinson in *The Common Cause*. 'By the 1830s, the now-much-extended republic was strictly a nation for whites.'[17]

The competing historical claims of Lepore and Parkinson hinge on the figure of Andrew Jackson, the military man of the people elected president by popular vote in 1828. 'The first principle of our system', said Jackson, 'is that the majority is to govern.'[18] But as Lepore subsequently acknowledges, Jackson was also a genocidal racist, whose Indian clearances resemble the Ottoman removal of the Armenians in 1915. Liberal democracy in the sense of competitive elections under universal suffrage was achieved in the US only in the late 1960s.

One curious aspect of the twisted history of democracy is that formal democratic institutions have occasionally been ceded from above, prior to any popular demand. Forerunners in this respect were the oligarchs of the Japanese Meiji Restoration, who in 1890 provided their country with a Constitution, a restrictive electoral system and a powerless Diet. The intention was to rally the population for the defence and strengthening of the realm, threatened by encroaching imperial predators. The 'reactive modernisers' of Japan may therefore be counted among the conservative nineteenth-century pioneers of what today has become a mainstream notion of democracy: that elections are not for popular power and social change, but for political management of the status quo, and for facilitating the development of national power.

### The meaning of democracy that people fought for

In other cases, democracy had to be won by the people, against ferocious opposition. There was a telling saying among the mid-nineteenth century German elite: '*Gegen Demokraten helfen nur Soldaten*' ('Against democrats, only soldiers help'). Or as the British historian and Whig cabinet minister Thomas Macaulay declared in the House of Commons on 3 May 1842: 'I believe universal suffrage would be fatal to all purposes for which government exists, and for which aristocracies and all other things exist, and that it is utterly incompatible with civilization ... I will oppose with every faculty I possess the proposition for universal suffrage.'[19]

Popular struggles for democracy had particular focal points in different parts of the world. Those in Europe were organized around class and class relations. Here, the foundational question was: 'What rights are the people entitled to?' The first mass mobilization for popular rule was the British Chartist movement against which Macaulay railed. It demanded universal male suffrage. The Second International broadened the demand to genuinely universal suffrage. Its 1893 Zürich congress unanimously adopted a resolution proclaiming 'the right to vote for everybody of mature age, without consideration of sex or race'.

The British pro-democracy campaign began in the wake of a disappointingly narrow extension of the franchise in 1832. Popular anger at the shortcomings of the 'Great Reform Act' were compounded by a harsh new liberal Poor Law consigning the poor and the unemployed to a kind of imprisonment in 'workhouses'. In February 1837 the London Working Men's Association adopted a petition to Parliament which became known as the People's Charter, with six demands: equal political representation of town and country, male suffrage, annual parliaments, no property qualifications for MPs, a secret ballot, regular sittings of Parliament throughout the year with attendance paid for. The Charter led to a nationwide, often militant mass campaign, mainly among skilled artisans and the working classes in general, though also attracting some radical middle-class support. It included a local insurrection (in Newport in southern Wales), and was imbricated, chaotically and without national leadership, in a large strike wave in 1842, which led to its defeat.

During the Chartist campaign, both the social democratic and the liberal-conservative conceptions of democracy got their early formulations. The former was expressed by one of the most prominent Chartist leaders, James Bronterre O'Brien: 'to establish democracy not only in the Government but throughout every industrial department of society'.[20] A public address of 1839 by a Women's Political Union in Newcastle put it more directly: 'pass the People's Charter into law and emancipate the white slaves of England'.[21] Critically commenting on the Charter's six points, the bourgeois *Manchester Guardian* stumbled on what has today become the standard view of liberal political science and journalism: the suffrage is 'merely an expedient for obtaining good government; *that,* and not the franchise, it is to which the public have a right.'[22] The American political scientist Samuel Huntington calls this a 'procedural concept of democracy', which by the 1970s had conquered all political science.[23] It is precisely this concept which is now in crisis.

The Chartists were defeated and their petition was rejected by the Westminster Parliament. But after a lull, the suffrage movement picked up again in 1867, pushing Benjamin Disraeli as leader of a Tory minority government to radically revise the original version of his electoral reform bill into a substantial extension of the franchise to about a third of adult men.

Disraeli's chameleonic politics are a brilliant example of the acrobatic agility of successful bourgeois politicians. In the parliamentary debate on the Chartist petition in 1839 Disraeli expressed sympathy for its signatories – later even writing a sympathetic novel, *Sybil* – but nevertheless voted against it meeting their demands. In 1866, he railed against a modest Liberal measure of franchise reform, warning that it would leave Parliament with 'no charm of tradition, no families of historic lineage; none of those great estates around which men rally when liberty is assailed'. A year later, now in government, he presented a rather similar Bill as a 'bulwark against democracy', adding: 'I trust it will never be the fate of this country to live under a democracy'. Yet two months on, defending his revised, much more generous Bill, he could only appeal to MPs to trust in his judgement that 'England is safe in the race of men who inhabit it ... safe in her national character ... in her fame'.[24]

The Belgian working class, and first of all its Wallonian coal miners, constituted the most heroic and dedicated fighters for democracy. Belgian labour staged a large economic-cum-political strike in 1891 in the mines of Borinage, Charleroi, and Liège, and three national general strikes for universal suffrage in 1893, 1902 and in 1913. The first general strike was violent and quasi-insurrectionary, and violently repressed. Seven democrats died and hundreds were wounded. It did achieve some electoral concessions, the substitution of a more limited system of plural votes for a property-based franchise. The second general strike was less revolutionary, reflecting a promise made to progressive liberals – who also demanded that the Workers Party should make clear that the strike did not demand political rights for women[25] – but it still involved unruly rebellious crowds. It was called off by the party leadership without any results, and became an issue of international debate due to a critical intervention by Rosa Luxemburg in the theoretical organ of German Social Democracy. The third general strike was peaceful and disciplined but delivered no more than a parliamentary Commission on electoral reform.

Sweden was one of the countries in Europe where the struggle for the political rights of the people was articulate and well organized, arising in a rapidly industrializing rural country with an archaic, only semi-parliamentary government – and, of course, a restricted suffrage. However, by the last quarter of the nineteenth century, Sweden was, together with the other Nordic countries, a popular society of extensive popular self-organization. While French universal male suffrage in 1848 was not enough to get a single farmer elected to the National Assembly in France, the Second Chamber of the post-1867 Swedish Diet was dominated by them, in the form of the Yeoman Party (*Lantmannapartiet*). Before social democracy and trade unionism took off in the late 1880s, Sweden was criss-crossed by large popular movements of religious dissent and of temperance, providing the mass base of democratic Liberalism.

Democracy, as universal suffrage, was the key political demand of Swedish Social Democracy, pursued in ceaseless campaigns, including a general strike (peaceful and disciplined) in 1902. A central feature of the Swedish labour movement's fight for democracy was the so-called Lill-Jans Resolution, first issued in 1987 at a meeting in the Lill-Jans forest on the outskirts of Stockholm and endorsed by innumerable meetings all over the country:

> As universal suffrage is an indispensable prerequisite for the people to become master in its own house in a legal manner and transform society after its needs; as the rapid granting of universal suffrage is the only road to a peaceful solution of the great social question; this meeting demands equal and direct right to vote and sufficient guarantees for the free exercise of this right in all political and municipal elections for all mature and reputable men.[26]

After his entry into Parliament in 1896, the Social Democratic leader Hjalmar Branting regularly presented bills demanding also female suffrage, in line with the resolutions of the Second International of 1891 and 1893. But a democratic breakthrough came only after the 1918 November Revolution in Berlin, when the Swedish Right found it safest to concede.

In the overseas colonies of the European powers, the twentieth century struggle for independence held out at least the promise not just of an elected sovereign national government, but of a differently constituted, egalitarian social order. As Jawaharlal Nehru argued in *Whither India?* (1933):

> What, then, are we driving at? Freedom? Swaraj? Independence? Dominion Status? Words which may mean much or little, or nothing at all. Again, whose freedom are we particularly striving for? ... India's immediate goal can ... only be considered in terms of the ending of the exploitation of her people. Politically it must mean independence ... economically and socially it must mean the ending of all special class privileges and vested interests ... Independence is a much-abused word and it hardly connotes what we are driving at. And yet, there is no other suitable word[27]

Nelson Mandela expressed a similar conception of post-colonial democracy at his Rivonia Trial:

> The structure and organization of early African society in this country ... greatly influenced the evolution of my political outlook. The land ... belonged to the whole tribe ... There were no classes, no rich or poor, no exploitation of man by man. All men were free and equal ... There was much in such a society that was primitive and insecure ... But in such a society are contained the seeds of revolutionary democracy in which none is held in slavery or servitude, and in which poverty, want and insecurity shall be no more.[28]

## Are all races people?

In the European settler states, 'race', in the sense of ethnic origin and physical appearance, has been more salient than class to the history of democracy. Male settlers were convinced that they were a people with rights. That was why they had seceded from the motherland, for violating or not fully upholding those rights. So, unlike in Europe, in the states of the Americas, Australia, New Zealand, South Africa, and Palestine, the main question of democracy has been, 'who are the people', which first of all means, 'are all races people'?

Where they were weak and relatively few in number, indigenous peoples were ignored for legal and political purposes, except as targets for violence and deportation. In the US, Indians were not counted in the census until 1870,[29] and were only granted citizenship in their land of ancestry in 1924, or about 150 years after the white settlers had proclaimed that 'all men were created equal'. To the founding Zionists, who were both Christians and Jews, Palestine was similarly 'a land without a people'.

In Hispanic America, indigenous peoples made up the majority of the population in the new Andean nations of Bolivia,

Ecuador and Peru, as well as in Guatemala, and nearly a third of the population in Mexico. As such, they could not be ignored. In the first wave of national Constitutions – none of which attained the sacrality of the US one – Indians were usually recognized as citizens with voting rights, unless they were servants or workers. But this relatively broad suffrage was actually a legacy of the Spanish Empire, and the settler nations came to restrict it in the course of the nineteenth century.[30] Already the liberal Spanish constitution of 1812 excluded 'Spaniards ... originating in Africa'[31], while Brazil was a slave society until 1888.

For demographic reasons 'race' became an even more central issue in Latin America than in the US and the British White Dominions, and for a time an obsession akin to South Africa. The people of the nation – the substance of popular sovereignty – were considered uncultivated and problematic by the ruling Creole elite. One solution, very influential in the last third of the nineteenth century and the first third of the twentieth, was to 'whiten' the people through European immigration or racial mixing, the latter banned by law in South Africa and the US but a recognized feature of Ibero-American society, with 'whitening' displayed as proof of social mobility in family portraits. The ideologies of this endogenous form of ethnic change ranged from the apologetic 'racial democracy' of the Brazilian anthropologist Gilberto Freyre to the utopian vision of a 'cosmic race' of *mestizaje* by the Education Minister of the Mexican Revolution, José Vasconcelos.[32]

Another solution issued from the republican ideal of an educated citizenry involved denying illiterate citizens the right to vote – a common practice of post-primary-wave constitutions in the region. As there were never sufficient resources and/or priorities for free universal education, a literacy requirement meant the effective exclusion, not only of the poorest but also of large chunks of 'undesirable' races, Indians, *Afrodescendentes* (as they are known in the region). In Brazil, more than half of the population was excluded from voting until the 1930s; in Chile, a quarter until 1945. The Latin American combination of settler racism and educational exclusivism created a very narrow bandwidth for electoral politics – the relatively peaceful civilian side of unstable states haunted by endless armed coups d'état.

In 1857, the race issue came before the US Supreme Court:

> The question is simply this: Can a Negro, whose ancestors were imported into this country, and sold as slaves, become a member of the political community formed and brought into existence by the Constitution of the United States ... ? ... We think that [Black people] are not included, and were not intended to be included, under the word 'citizen' in the Constitution ... On the contrary, they were at the time considered as a subordinate and inferior class of beings ... And whether emancipated or not, yet remained subject to [the dominant race's] authority.[33]

Contrary to intention, the notorious *Dred Scott v. Sanford* case further inflamed the slavery cleavage in the US, and was overruled by the Fourteenth Amendment following the Civil War. To ensure that all adult male citizens had the right to vote required yet another amendment, passed in 1870, prohibiting the federal government and each state from denying a citizen the right to vote based on 'race, colour, or previous condition of servitude'. However, after the end of Reconstruction in 1877, racist exclusion soon returned in the South under cover of various legal fictions, facilitated by the lack of a universalistic democratic tradition in the US asserting the political rights of all citizens. In 1896, in the case of *Plessy v. Ferguson*, the Supreme Court ruled that 'distinctions based on colour' were constitutional, legalizing racial segregation in all walks of life, from schools to shops, restaurants and theatres.

On the steps at the Lincoln Memorial in Washington DC on

28 August 1963, Martin Luther King told the rulers of the US, as well as his own followers:

> We have come to this hallowed spot to remind America of the fierce urgency of now. This is no time to engage in the luxury of cooling off or to take the tranquilizing drug of gradualism. Now is the time to make real the promises of democracy ... There will be neither rest nor tranquillity in America until the Negro is granted his citizenship rights. The whirlwinds of revolt will continue to shake the foundations of our nation until the bright days of justice emerge. [34]

Malcolm X, in his last major speech in December 1964, set out his view of the African-American movement for democracy:

> Our objective is complete freedom, complete justice, complete equality, by any means necessary. That never changes. Complete and immediate recognition and respect as human beings, that doesn't change. I don't care what you belong to, you still want that recognition and respect as a human being. But you have changed your methods from time to time on how you go about getting it.

> This is the richest country on earth and there's poverty, there's bad housing, there's slums, there's inferior education... What they are using to solve their problem in Africa and Asia is not capitalism. So what you and I should do is find out what they are using to get rid of poverty and all the other negative characterics of a rundown society.[35]

Voting only became a legal right in all of the US the following year, with the Voting Rights Act, and was effective only after a Civil Rights movement voter-registration campaign in Selma Alabama had been subjected to a ferocious repression by the state organs of Alabama, causing national uproar. Three people had been killed.[36]

**Table 2.** Voting in the Americas, 1850–1940: Percentage of the
population voting

| US | 1850 12.9 | 1889 18.3 | 1920 25.1 | 1940 37.8 |
|---|---|---|---|---|
| Canada | 1867 7.7 | 1878 12.9 | 1917 20.5 | 1940 41.1 |
| | | | | |
| Argentina | | 1916 9.0 | 1928 12.8 | 1937 15.0 |
| Brazil | 1894 2.2 | 1914 2.4 | 1930 5.7 | |
| Chile | 1869 1.6 | 1881 3.1 | 1920 4.4 | 1938 9.4 |
| Colombia | | 1918 6.8 | 1930 11.1 | 1936 5.9 |
| Ecuador | 1856 0.1 | 1888 2.8 | | 1940 3.3 |
| Mexico | | 1920 6.6 | | 1940 11.8 |
| Uruguay | | | 1920 13.8 | 1940 19.7 |

Source: S. Engerman and K. Sokoloff, 'Inequality, Institutions and Differential Paths of
Growth among New World economies', paper for the MacArthur Research Network, 2001,
Table 5; American Pew Research Center, 8 November 2014.

## The other half of democracy: Votes for women

The feminist struggle for democracy first developed in the
United States. There had been some feminist voices in the
French revolutionary upsurges of 1789, 1848 and 1871, but
they were shoved aside, silenced, arrested or executed, leaving
no direct heritage. The first feminist campaign succeeded in a
New York State Act on married women's property rights. In
the aftermath of that, two Quaker women issued invites to a
Women's Rights Convention at Seneca Falls, NY, in 1848. This
was the launch of a democratic mass movement, which had to
fight for seventy years to succeed. Its famous Declaration is a
resounding, radical call to battle:

> We hold these truths to be self-evident: that all men and women
> are created equal ...
> The history of mankind is a history of repeated injuries and
> usurpations on the part of man toward woman, having in direct
> object the establishment of an absolute tyranny over her. To
> prove this, let facts be submitted to a candid world.

He has never permitted her to exercise her inalienable right to the elective franchise.

He has compelled her to submit to laws, in the formation of which she had no voice.

He has withheld from her rights which are given to the most ignorant and degraded men – both natives and foreigners.

Having deprived her of this first right of a citizen, the elective franchise, thereby leaving her without representation in the halls of legislation, he has oppressed her on all sides.

He has made her, if married, in the eye of the law, civilly dead ...

He has endeavoured, in every way that he could, to destroy her confidence in her own powers, to lessen her self-respect, and to make her willing to lead a dependent and abject life.

Now, in view of this entire disfranchisement of one-half the people of this country, their social and religious degradation – in view of the unjust laws above mentioned, and because women do feel themselves aggrieved, oppressed, and fraudulently deprived of their most sacred rights, we insist that they have immediate admission to all the rights and privileges which belong to them as citizens of the United States.[37]

A peculiar variant of the typical settler question, 'Who are the people?', was rolled out in Canada in the 1920s: 'Are women persons?'. According to the British North America Act of 1867, Canada's imperial constitution, persons could be nominated for and elected to public office. In the early 1920s a woman had been nominated to the Canadian Senate. Was she a person? The wisdom of British common law had clarified the issue in 1876: 'Women are persons in matters of pain and penalties, but not persons in matters of rights and privileges.' In somewhat more diplomatic terms, this view was re-affirmed by the Canadian Supreme Court in 1928. However, in the British Empire there was one more instance of appeal, the Privy Council in London, which in 1929 graciously accorded personhood to women.[38]

The feminist struggle for democracy developed along two lines, one a bourgeois movement centred in the United States, strong also in Britain and the White Dominions, drawing upon non-established Protestant Christianity, a powerful Temperance movement, and access to male Liberalism. The other was socialist, addressing working-class women, linked to the Second International and its Social Democratic member parties – above all the German one, the largest and the one most committed to the women's cause. Party leader August Bebel's 1883 book *Die Frau und der Sozialismus* (Woman and Socialism) became a bestseller among the popular classes of Germany, running to thirty-four editions by 1903.

An attempt to connect the two feminist currents at a congress in Paris in 1900 foundered on different views of class issues.[39] Both currents had to navigate their way through national patriarchies. The first international breakthroughs came in the wake of the two world wars. The next one was the UN Women's Conference in Mexico City in 1974.[40]

Tracing the roots of modern democracy in this way, to popular struggles against the forces of anti-democracy, it becomes clear that people were fighting for something very different from the political game investigated by current political scientists. They wanted rule by the people because they wanted autonomy, dignity, civic rights and egalitarian socio-economic change. This is the yardstick against which contemporary democracies should be measured.

## II. The Loveless Marriage of Capitalism and Democracy

Capital has no interest in democracy; on the contrary, it has good reason to resist having to face masses of workers with political rights, including even the right to elect a workers' government. And resist it did, supported by all the ideologues of private property rights, from John Stuart Mill onwards.

Nevertheless, after decades, sometimes more than a century, of resistance, liberal democracy did finally become the norm in capitalist countries. How did this come to pass?

This was the research question of a then young social scientist more than forty years ago. My answer briefly summed up, was that democracy emerged out of contingent contradictions of capitalism, often in relation to external state wars, and under situations of popular pressure making democratic concession appear a lesser evil than popular rebellion or revolution. I developed this argument in the original version of 'The Rule of Capital and the Rise of Democracy'.

What happened in the subsequent relationship between capitalism and democracy? A recent book by two prominent institutional economists, Torben Iversen and David Soskice, presents it as a fairy-tale ending, where the couple lived together happily ever after.[41] The subject needs to be revisited with some historical realism.

## Interwar dating

In the aftermath of World War I, organized capital was still undecided on its best political partner, and more often linked up with anti-democratic regimes than with democratic ones. Fascist Germany and Italy, Salazar's Portugal and Franco's Spain, Vichy France and pre-Anschluss Austria, the conservative authoritarian regimes of Eastern Europe, racist South Africa, and military regimes from Japan to Argentina all offered good opportunities for profit while pursuing their own goals. Nowhere did capital put up any demand for democracy: there was no capitalist '20th of July', the heroic attempt to get rid of Hitler by a section of the German military aristocracy.

In central Europe, Hitler and Mussolini promised a great future for national capitalism, and to keep labour in its place. The support of business leaders such as Hugenberg, Kirdorf, Schacht and Thyssen was crucial to Hitler's acceptance by the conservative establishment around President Hindenburg, smoothing his rise to power. Partnership with big business was decisive both for his industrial genocide (the gas from IG Farben) and for the arming of his war machine. At a meeting on 20 February 1933 with Göring and Hitler, who asked for contributions to the NSDAP campaign for the elections of 5 March, which if the party won, Göring said, would be the last election for ten years, perhaps even for a hundred years, the captains of German business were all there, paying up, the owners or executives of Agfa, Allianz, BASF, Bayer, IG Farben, Krupp, Opel, Siemens, Telefunken, and others. Twenty-four of them.[42] There was admiration of Fascism and Nazism in some Anglo-Saxon business circles, as Henry Ford and the British press tycoon Lord Rothermere exemplify, while pluto-cratic liberalism equipped with an anti-trade union judiciary remained an attractive option in the US, the world's rising great power.

The outcome of World War Two ended the political dating period of capital. Hitler, Mussolini and Tojo were all defeated and ignominiously dead. The fate of Berlin, Tokyo and Hiroshima made clear that Fascism and militarism no longer offered good prospects for capital accumulation. On the other hand, in the immediate aftermath of the conflict, capital was not everywhere a respectable suitor for democrats, particularly not in the post-Fascist countries. The February 1947 Ahlener Programme of West German Christian Democracy was anti-capitalist in spirit: 'The capitalist economic system has not been fair [gerecht] to the state or to the social interests of the German people. The substance and goal of the new social and economic order can no longer be the capitalist striving for profit and power, but only the well-being of our people.' The Italian Constitution, meanwhile, declared the country a 'demo-cratic republic, founded on work', with a duty 'to remove the economic and social obstacles which by limiting the freedom and equality of citizens, prevent the full development of the human person and the effective participation of all workers in the political, economic and social organisation of the country'.

British voters trounced the war hero Churchill in the 1945 election and voted in a Labour government aiming at a socialist Britain. Eastern Europe's only pre-war democracy, Czechoslovakia, was also on a socialist course, even before the Communist seizure of power in 1948. In France, Socialists and Communists attracted the support of nearly half of the electorate. Early post-war Scandinavian Social Democracy preferred a singlehood of socio-economic reform to a liaison with capital, which campaigned vigorously against it without much electoral success. Japan was under US occupation, but initially a radical New Deal occupation refrained from interfering with strong indigenous socialist currents. In China, although the evidence is hardly conclusive, it seems that urban democrats more often preferred the Communists and their 'New Democracy' to the corrupt and incompetent Guomindang. Only in the US was there hardly any alternative to capital, but the governing New Deal Democrats did not have much love for it.

## Cold War marriage

The radical dreams of 1945 quickly faded, however. With the outbreak of the Cold War, capital had only one possible consort left, at least in the Global North. Marshall Aid investment in war-ravaged Europe gave US-led capitalism some much-needed popular appeal. Capital could count on the support of European social democracy and North American organized labour as well as on the middle classes. Put together, these elements formed the basis of the NATO coalition. Democracy and developed capitalism finally married under the auspices of the Cold War. On the whole it has been a loveless marriage.

Outside the capitalist core, on the other hand, other suitors could still be found. Entrance criteria to the 'Free World' club was lower even than in Natoland, which admitted nondemocracies like Portugal and Turkey even if it couldn't, upon northern European resistance, stomach Franco's Spain. The racist thugs of South Africa, the killing and torturing generals of Latin America and Pakistan, the civilian oligarchs of Malaysia and the Philippines, and the Arab oil sheikhs, were all perfectly acceptable partners for capital.

As the post-war decades rolled on, and movements for egalitarian and participatory democracy arose within the Western fortress, the brains of developed capitalism began to prepare for a separation between capitalism and democracy. David Rockefeller brought together academics, government officials and businessmen in the Trilateral Commission in 1973, which commissioned a report on 'The Crisis of Democracy'. The crisis in question was not the bloody reversal of democracy in Latin America – the coup in Chile; another coup on the horizon in Argentina; Brazil already under military dictatorship; Mexico reeling from the massacre of Tlatelolco. For as the doyen of extreme twentieth-century liberalism Friedrich von Hayek told *El Mercurio*, mouthpiece of the Chilean bourgeoisie: 'Personally, I prefer a liberal dictator to a democratic government without liberalism.'[43]

Rather, the 'crisis' concerned what Samuel Huntington, one of the report's authors, termed an 'excess of democracy', occasioned by the 'democratic surge' of the 1960s. As his French co-author Michel Crozier explained, European democracies 'were built on a subtle screening of participants and demands; and if we can talk of overload … it is because this traditional model of screening and government-by-distance has gradually broken down'. The conclusion to the report elaborated: 'The pursuit of the democratic virtues of equality and individualism has led to delegitimation of authority generally … The democratic expansion of political participation and involvement has created an "overload" on government and the imbalanced expansion of government activities.'[44] In this spirit, after 1980, a neoliberal rollback began to re-insulate governments from popular demands, influence and participation. These measures took the form of privatizations, regulation by technocratic bodies such as central banks, and statutory budget constraints at national as well as European level.[45] The most drastic example of the latter has been the Brazilian cap on public spending for the period 2016–36. Neoliberal capitalism has in effect put a chastity belt on democracy.

## Restoration

The restoration of capitalism in Eastern Europe and the Soviet Union from 1989 provides further insights into the loveless relationship between capitalism and democracy. The anti-Communist rebellions were not movements for social justice but rather for political liberties and, in several cases, national sovereignty. Significantly, the central political concept of the movements, besides ethnic nationalism, was not democracy, with its connotation of popular power, but 'civil society', best captured in its classical German formulation, *bürgerliche Gesellschaft*, with its intrinsic ambiguity of civic society and bourgeois society. It was a vision of civilized, intellectual citizens, unbothered by anything economic as well as by the state. The great West German political scientist Klaus von Beyme called civil society 'the last ideology of the old [Eastern European] *intelligentsia*', and noticed shrewdly that 'just [*schlichte*] taking over Western democracy had little *sex appeal*'.[46]

The main point in this context is that the economic system, the existing as well as a future one, was below the attention of the anti-Communist movements and their ideologues. Von Beyme talks of the 'alienation from the economy [*Wirtschaftsfremdheit*]' of the Eastern European intelligentsia.[47] And no one demonstrated in Eastern Europe in 1989–91 under a banner of capitalism. The massive people's movements were about people's freedom, people's national independence, not about people's power.

Except for among a few rightwing economists catapulted into power, like Leszek Balcerowicz in Poland and Václav Klaus in Czechia, capitalism was no respectable groom to civil society or democracy; it had to be smuggled in by night, through a backdoor. The principal Western spokesperson of Polish *Solidarnosz*, Timothy Garton Ash, has summarized the Polish story:

> Among Solidarity's economic spokesmen during the Round Table and the electoral campaign, the cautious, gradualist 'market socialist' approach had been predominant. ... Yet almost the first remark [Tadeusz Mazowiecki] made as prime minister was: 'I am looking for my Ludwig Erhard'. He found him in a radical liberal economist Leszek Balcerowicz – an Erhard without the cigar.[48]

Erhard, a right-wing liberal, had been West Germany's minister of economic affairs after the Second World War, from 1949–1963. His latter-day incarnation, Balcerowicz, rapidly put together a 'shock therapy' plan for re-introducing capitalism in Poland, and had it cleared in Washington before presenting it to the Polish Parliament.

Post-Communists embraced democracy, but the socioeconomic system of Post-Communism was not decided democratically. It was decided instead behind the backs of ordinary people, and with disdain for the otherwise much-celebrated 'civil society'. A large British survey at the end of 1993 of popular opinion in the former Soviet Union (FSU) and in East Central Europe (ECE) (Czechia, Slovakia, Hungary) revealed huge non-capitalist majorities.

Three quarters of people in the FSU thought car factories should be owned by the state and two thirds thought the same of computer manufacturers, whereas in ECE, the numbers were 38 and 46 per cent respectively. In the FSU, 46 per cent of the population named the state as their favourite employer;

in ECE, the figure was 34 per cent. In both regions, only 13 per cent preferred private employers, with only a fifth saying they preferred a foreign employer. Nine out of ten in both post-Communist regions thought the state should be the main provider of health care; in the FSU the same proportion also held that the state was responsible for jobs, and should set the prices of basic goods and services. On the last two issues, the ECE majority for the state, compared to 'private businesses and the market economy', ranged between 72 and 81 per cent. In both regions, eight out of ten thought that the state should be the main provider of housing.[49]

The study also made another noteworthy discovery, the wide discrepancy between the peoples of Post-Communism and their politicians, their members of Parliament. In both regions there were popular majorities for 'socialist values' – of equality, state property, and collective welfare: large majorities in Russia and Ukraine, smaller ones in Czechia and Hungary. Among MPs, on the other hand, half of all Russian and Ukrainian MPs and only a quarter of those in Czechia and Hungary had values similar to the popular majority.[50]

Treuhand, the institution set up for the privatization and capitalization of the East German economy, became the most hated institution of post-Communist Germany, after sending three million Germans into unemployment by 1993, and transferring 88 per cent of East German property to West German firms. By the end of 1994, the name of the institution had to be changed, for the remaining decade of its existence.[51] Little wonder, then, that thirty years after the crumbling of the not very democratic East German Communism, 52 per cent of East Germans are little or not at all satisfied [zufrieden] with the functioning of democracy in Germany, while 48 per cent are very or 'rather' satisfied.[52]

## III. Mutations and Perversions

Democracy has had civilizing effects on capital, in particular in the US and Scandinavia in the wake of the Depression, and more generally in the Global North during the golden age of advanced industrial capitalism from the end of WWII to circa 1980. But no democracy has subverted any capitalism, nor altered its structure and dynamics. In the liaison between capitalism and democracy, capitalism has transformed democracy more than democracy has transformed capitalism. We shall now look into the role of capitalism in the mutations of democracy.

Democracy was once a matter of life and death. Popular demonstrators have risked their lives for it, striking workers have died for it, civil rights activists have been murdered for it, suffragettes have been jailed for it. Why did people commit themselves in this no holds barred way? Because for them fighting for democracy was fighting for social change and social justice.

What a perceptive political scientist now calls 'really existing democracies'[53] is, in a way, an apt parallel to the 'actually existing socialism' of the 1970s and 1980s, with a similar relationship to the ideals of the historical fighters for democracy and socialism – then expressing a resigned or cynical coping with living in the decaying ruins of the aspirations and ambitions of the October Revolution.

The game of democracy was defined by the conservative Austrian-American economist Josef Schumpeter 'as institutional arrangements for arriving at political decisions in which individuals acquire the power to decide by means of a competitive struggle for the people's vote.'[54] It was validated as the consensus of mainstream political science by Samuel P. Huntington.[55] One of the greatest empirical researchers of democracy, Adam Przeworski, has added another twist to the game, 'alternation', arguing that a regime of free competitive elections is no democracy until an incumbent has peacefully ceded power.[56] The logic of the hardnosed variables investigator can be followed. The implication, however, is that in the last instance, democracy is a pendulum, moving between A and B, or even between left and right, but hardly forward or backward. This is the kind of democracy currently in crisis, a game of professionals which sections of the populace are increasingly fed up with.

Democracy, in the sense of a competitive leadership sport, a professional game, has developed two perverse effects, non-representative policy-making and manipulated elections.

## Non-representation

Representation is a key idea of modern democracy, in which the people elect representatives to govern on their behalf. What happens to democracy if the elected representatives in fact represent other interests and preferences than their electorate? There is now hard evidence that they do, more often than not.

One of the major recent advances of political science has been the systematic empirical study of the relations between voters' policy preferences and democratic political decision-making. The trailblazers were American, Larry Bartels and Martin Giles,[57] and their investigations have spawned replicas in European countries, with similar patterns of results, although not necessarily as dramatic. Bartels found, for instance, that in 1989–95 and 2011–13 the policy opinions of the bottom third of the income ladder had no impact at all on the US Senate.[58] Giles' study of US government policies in 1981–2002 found that when the preferences of income groups diverge, those of the bottom 70 per cent don't count at all, and the government responds only to the richest 10 per cent.[59]

One of the most interesting political replicas of Bartels and Giles is a Swedish one made by two political scientists at Gothenburg University. Sweden is a society with considerably less inequality than the US, and has a political system where parties and candidates are not dependent on rich donor financing. Social Democracy is both the electorally dominant and financially strongest conmponent (due to union support) of its proportional electoral system. Nevertheless, the same class hierarchy of government policy responsiveness holds as in the US, although the scale is more modest. Magnus Persson and Mikael Gilljam have looked at the relations between public policy opinion and government policies for the period 1956 to 2014. When the opinions of income groups diverged, those supported by the richest ten per cent (the ninetieth percentile more precisely) were implemented in 20 per cent of cases, while those preferred by the median voter (the fiftieth percentile) or by the bottom tenth percentile were governmentally heeded about 9 per cent of the time. Social Democratic and bourgeois governments alike implemented only 9 per cent of the preferences of low-income earners, whereas 16 per cent of the demands of the rich (the ninetieth percentile) were implemented by Social Democratic governments, compared to a figure of 26 per cent under bourgeois governments.[60] Under both types of government, the bottom half of the population had to take a back seat to the richest 10 per cent.

The reasons for this systemic non-responsiveness of liberal democracies to popular opinion whenever it diverges from the worldview of the richest 10 per cent run deeper than electoral finance. One major cause is the ambience in which contemporary politicians are embedded: a predominantly upper middle class environment to which the bottom two thirds of the population have little access, a club of fellow privileged professional politicians, of resourceful lobby groups, of think tanks and policy wonks, and powerful media journalists, with an inner circle of advisers, strategic consultants, agenda planners, and communications officers. Popular access, through party, movement and constituency, has great difficulties penetrating this carapace of professional political poker players, with the exception of the local issues of single-member constituencies.

Many politicians seem to have lost the capacity to speak the language of ordinary people. A perspicacious and critical political observer like the British political scientist Colin Crouch explained the rise of Jeremy Corbyn (of whom Crouch was no fan), against all political odds and without any particular rhetorical skills, as (largely) due to his ability to speak the vernacular of non-politicians.[61]

A second reason, perhaps, is the exhaustion of social democratic or social liberal reform, and political self-limitation to the management of capitalism. For that purpose, the knowledge, interests, and opinions of the richest 10 per cent are clearly more relevant than the wishes of the bottom 70 per cent.

### The business of managing elections

Across the populated continents, elections used to be 'managed' by local landowners and clergy, fêting their flock and herding them to the ballot box (or by the Ministry of the Interior and its prefects, as in the interwar Balkans). Now their running has become a global business, not always as effective, but much more widely influential.

In an undercover video about the successful electoral campaigns of Kenya's Uhuru Kenyatta, Mark Turnbull, managing director of Cambridge Analytica, can be heard saying, 'We have rebranded the entire party twice, written their manifesto, done two successful rounds of 50,000 participant surveys. Then we'd written all the speeches and we'd staged the whole thing – so just about every element of his campaign'. Cambridge Analytica was a British company, unrelated to the university its name invokes, which specialized in personal data trawling and dirty campaigning, not only for figures like Trump and Ted Cruz, but also for politicians in Brazil, India, Kenya, Malaysia and Mexico.

Cambridge Analytica's illegal data-trawling finally forced it to close down, but it is only one of the most brazen examples of an ongoing subversion of democracy, by professional electoral manipulators. In the US, professional commercial political campaigning goes back to the 1930s. In Europe it was introduced by Margaret Thatcher in 1979, when she hired Saatchi & Saatchi to oust Labour in 1979.

The manager of the Saatchi campaigns was Tim Bell, who later worked for the National Coal Board against the striking miners in 1984, and for the Pinochetista Presidential candidate Hernán Büchi – who lost in 1989 – as well as for the Pinochet Foundation. In 1996, he was the Saatchi & Saatchi man organizing Yeltsin's electoral victory in Russia. In the 2000s he worked for the Saudi government and its defence against allegations of bribing, and in the 2010s he campaigned for the Gupta brothers trying to capture the state of South Africa.

This fauna of electoral predators holds many more specimens. One is the Miami Venezuelan Juan José Rendón, who boasts of winning the presidential campaigns of Juan Manuel Santos (Colombia) twice, Enrique Peña Nieto (Mexico) and Lobo Sosa and Juan Orlando Hernández, the previous and current presidents of post-coup Honduras – all of them conservatives. In 2013, Rendón and his candidate Capriles lost to Nicolás Maduro in Venezuela. In 2020 he was Juan Guido's strategist behind a farcical attempt to kidnap Maduro by US mercenaries.

Paul Manafort, once Donald Trump's electoral manager, is another example. He started his consultancy career as manager of Ronald Reagan's southern (White race) campaign, and then he worked for a long time as a lobbyist for an international cabinet of horrors: for the US stooge in Angola, Jonas Savimbi; for the Saudi government; for Ferdinand Marcos and General Mobutu; for the ruler of Equatorial Guinea and several other African governments; and for the Pakistani Intelligence Services. His most successful electoral intervention was in Ukraine, managing the presidential tilt of Viktor Yanukovich in 2010.

Another characteristic figure in the business is Sir Lynton Crosby, an Australian operative, knighted by David Cameron, who with his firm CTF Partners has run several Tory campaigns, and who has also worked for the Saudi Arabian and Zimbabwean governments, the super-corrupt ex–prime minister of Malaysia Najib Razak and others in the same class. Crosby's righthand man, Isaac Levido, successfully managed recent campaigns by Scott Morrison in Australia and Boris Johnson in the UK.

The extent to which elections are decided by spin doctors and international managers and 'consultants' is still unknown, although it is certain to be substantially below 100 per cent. Clearly this is a phenomenon geared to subverting the meaning of democratic elections, and of public opinion. 'Beneath the cornucopia of the digital public sphere we are shocked to discover a labyrinth of profit-driven algorithms', as the contemporary historian Adam Tooze has put it.[62] With the densification of unidentifiable social media and the appropriation of ever growing big personal data, the manipulation of opinion and of elections is likely to increase.

This is where democracy has arrived in the early twenty-first century: global businessmen run elections, and regardless of who is elected, the dreams, demands and complaints of the bottom half or seventy per cent of the population are ignored. The hopeful thing is that this democracy is widely acknowledged to be in crisis.

## IV. Abandonments

Under the neoliberal dispensation, democratic capitalist societies have been torn apart by a new political economy. As people have become 'populists', a foul-smelling aberration beyond the pale of polite society, varyingly large sectors of society have been more or less abandoned or excluded, and treated mainly as objects of surveillance. I shall here highlight four processes of desertion and exclusion in neoliberal democracies. One hits society's most vulnerable, who have become democracy's foundlings. The second is the lethal abandonment of the populations of the post-industrial peripheries. Pushing down the bottom half of the population is a third tendency, and fourthly there is the abandonment of the middle class by elites and the high bourgeoisie.

## Democracy's foundlings

A foundling was an abandoned infant, left to the mercy of private charity. Foundling hospitals were institutions of the medieval Catholic Church, which expanded in the eighteenth and nineteenth centuries of early European urbanization and capitalist industrialization, with their concomitant proletarianization and extra-marital pregnancies. I use the metaphor to highlight contemporary democratic states' abandonment of their most vulnerable and undesirable, leaving them to be picked up by private charity.

A 2019 UN report by Philip Alston, from whom I once learnt human rights law at a distance, provided an unusually blunt summary of what is going on in the UK under Tory democracy: 'a systematic immiseration of a significant part of the British population'. A fifth of the population, 14 million people, was found to be living in poverty once housing costs and child care are taken into account. Of these, 1.5 million had experienced destitution in 2017, defined as having less than £10 a day after housing costs or going without at least two essentials such as shelter, food, heat, light, clothing or toiletries during a one-month period.[63]

Child poverty has been one of the most felt accomplishments of the political Right in the developed world over the past four decades. The Conservative administrations of Margaret Thatcher and John Major made a lasting impact on British child poverty, increasing it from 13 to 30 per cent. In the US it climbed from 21 to 31 per cent between 1974 and 2016, and in Germany from 8 to 29 per cent. In France it has now reached 19 per cent.[64] Little wonder that social mobility is declining and windows of opportunity are closing, when an increasing number of children have to grow up in relative poverty, and the ongoing privatization makes good education increasingly out of reach for the non-rich.

The outcasts of contemporary democratic capitalism are increasingly becoming dependent on charity to survive. Not only in the US, with its regular food charities as well as its degrading food stamps system, but also in the welfare states of Europe. In 2014, a British All-Party Parliamentary Group on food poverty announced that 'hunger stalks Britain', and a year later that 'hunger is now regarded as a "fact of life" in the UK's poorest communities'. By then the Trussell Trust's network of 400 hundred food banks were giving out more than a million three-day-emergency food parcels. NHS statistics recorded 7,366 hospital admissions for malnutrition from August 2014 to July 2015.[65] The background to this deplorable state of affairs lies in the effects on employment of the financial crash of 2008, the large-scale cuts to social spending by the Conservative Cameron-Osborne government, and their brutal and incompetent implementation by the social services, leaving needy citizens waiting for weeks and months for the meagre benefits they were entitled to.

Spain was hit hard by the crash of 2008, which threw masses of workers into unemployment and those with mortgages out into the street. Many became reliant on a widespread foodbank network, part of which developed out of the *Indignados* protest movement of 15 May 2011.[66] Sweden, by contrast was hurt only minimally and briefly, but nevertheless, food poverty emerged there too in the 2010s. In 2018 the Salvation Army distributed 27,000 food parcels a month. Rich Germany has many poor, and 1.5 million people resort to food charities recurrently.[67]

## Abandoned territories, avoidable deaths

Capitalist deindustrialization has created abandoned territories of the un(der)employed, new peripheries of a post-industrial economy pulsating elsewhere. The North of England and France, the English Midlands, the East of Germany and the Ruhr region in the west of the country, American Rust-belt, sometimes broadened to small-town America in general,[68] and the northern and mid-west inland areas of Sweden: all these areas have been left behind. The devastated parts of the UK are more numerous and more desolate than those in the rest of Europe. While Inner London, the most privileged area of Europe, hoards almost six times the national average of GDP per capita, among the fifteen most abandoned territories of Europe (with about half of the national average GDP per capita), eleven are British, two are German, one is Italian, and one is French, the island of Réunion in the Indian Ocean.[69] No other national elite has abandoned so much of its territory, and their populations, as the British. Observers have taken notice of these regions mainly on account of their unconventional voting behaviour, mostly rightwing, replacing old, rational leftwing class politics – Front National, Trumpism, Brexit: major challenges to progressive, egalitarian politics, to which we shall return below. Here I shall highlight a much less noticed aspect of the peripheries: deaths from social neglect.

British medical statistics include a very valuable indicator of unequal lives. It is called 'avoidable deaths', which 'are all those defined as preventable, amenable (treatable) or both'. Rates of death are adjusted for the different age-composition of the populations investigated. A quarter of all UK deaths in 2017 were avoidable, rising to a third of all deaths of children and young people. Avoidable deaths occur everywhere, from accidental injuries for example, even in places like Surrey and Chelsea. But they are typical of areas outside the centres of affluence. A mortality map of the UK is remarkably similar to a pre-2019 electoral map, with dark, high mortality areas across the North East in Durham and Teesside in particular, and another very dark band lying eastwards from Blackpool and Merseyside to Humberside, a Midlands belt. Parts of London appear as dark spots in an otherwise bright southern landscape. All of Wales is rather dark, the major population areas in the South and the North of the country particularly so.

In absolute numbers, avoidable deaths decreased from 2001 to 2013, but stalled after that. The relative gap between the 10 per cent most deprived areas and 10 per cent least deprived widened among women from 3 times higher mortality among women to 3.9 times, and among men from 3.5 to 4.5.[70]

The most telling metric is probably that of treatable deaths. A resident of Bradford runs 3.4 times the risk of dying from a treatable cause than someone in Surrey Heath. Other high risk NHS areas are Manchester, Blackpool, Hull and Liverpool. In London, the risks of treatable death are twice as high in Hackney, Barking and Dagenham, Southwark, and Lambeth as they are in West London.

In the US, Elias Nosrati has found that in the Rustbelt, the lives of the poorest quarter of the population are 1.5 years shorter than those in the bottom quarter in other states.[71] The middle-aged White working class in the Rustbelt has been the largest victim of the ruthless selling of opioid painkillers leading to the highest drug overdose death rates in the US: 57.8 per 100,000 in West Virginia in 2007, 46.8 in Ohio, and 44.3 in Pennsylvania, compared to a national rate of 21.7.[72]

Likewise in Sweden, life is becoming shorter in peripheral municipalities. In the ten municipalities with the shortest life expectancy in the country, between 2008–12 and between 2013–17, life expectancy (at birth) among men declined in seven municipalities, and among women in nine municipalities. In two northern municipalities life expectancy fell by three years.[73]

The peripheral populations are socially part of a larger (w)hole of contemporary liberal democracy, the bottom half of the population.

## Pushing down the lower half

A widespread effect of the neoliberal turn since about 1980 has been a cut in the national income share of the bottom 50 per cent. It is a relative push-down, allowing for some minor absolute income increase over time as well as long-term stagnation. In neocapitalist Russia, somewhat more than the bottom 40 per cent of the population had lower incomes in 2016 than in 1989.[74] Table 3 provides further examples.

The neoliberal push-down of the lower half of the population in rich capitalist democracies exhibits three interesting patterns, plus one case representing the recurrent phenomenon of exceptions. One pattern, illustrated above by Poland and Russia, is related to the restoration of capitalism, which, of course, implied a restoration of the social order of capitalist 'normalcy', with workers and peasants at the bottom and the urban intelligentsia elevated into an upper middle class. Another pattern is the achievement of the vanguard battalions of the new global Right, the Reaganite US and Thatcherite

**Table 3.** Declining Share of National Income of the Bottom Half of the Population, from Late Twentieth Century Peak to c. 2014

|  | Percentage point decline | Peak year |
|---|---|---|
| France | 0.5 | 1983 |
| Germany | 6.6 | 2001 |
| Poland | 9.2 | 1988 |
| Russia | 12.7 | 1990 |
| Sweden | 5.6 | 1980 |
| UK | 6.8 | 1978 |
| US | 7.5 | 1978 |

Note: The Swedish date refers to disposable income after transfers and taxes, the others to income after cash transfers but before taxes.

Sources: Sweden: Statistics Sweden, *Inkomstfördelningen 1975–2013* (2015) and *Fördelning inkomster 2011–2017* (2019). The rest: F. Alvaredo, et al., *World Inequality Report 2018*, part II, Figure 2.3.2, and World Inequality Database. Alvaredo, et al., report a West German fall of 11 percentage points between 1965 and 1974; this looks suspiciously high, and does not seem to be supported by other literature on the period.

UK. Less expected, perhaps, is the significance of the self-damaging right-wing turn of European Social Democracy, as demonstrated by Germany and Sweden. In both countries Social Democratic governments gave their own electoral base a 'haircut', as the IMF economists used to say.

The new Social Democratic course started in Sweden in 1982, radicalizing in the 1990s and the first half of the noughties; the German one started in 2003. The background was an economic crisis, interpreted by the Social Democratic leadership as mainly due to workers earning too much and social entitlements being too generous. Swedish 1980s deregulation of the credit market and scrapping of capital controls created a financial bubble, which led to a much more severe crisis in the early 1990s. Despite its obvious origin it was interpreted in the same way as before – too much union power, too much generosity of social benefits, and too much taxation of wealth, inheritance, and capital income. The push-down of the lower half of the population was intensified. In Germany, Gerhardt Schroeder's Agenda 2010, endorsed by a Social Democratic (SPD) congress majority of two thirds in 2003, aimed at creating a large low-wage segment of the labour market by drastically cutting unemployment insurance and social benefits.[75]

Both programmes succeeded in putting national capitalism on a new, more profitable path, and have been continued and expanded by bourgeois successors. Both also initiated the dramatic decline of Social Democracy, most dramatically of the German SPD – currently a third- or fourth-rate 15-per cent party – while the Swedish Social Democratic Party (SAP) is clinging on to an increasingly threatened first-rank position, with support at half the size of what it had in the decades before the neoliberal escapade. The lower half of the population has taken notice of the current priorities of the Social Democratic leadership. In opinion polls at the end of 2019, Swedish Social Democracy was virtually level with the xenophobic Sweden Democrats.

In a political sense, French Socialism and Communism are part of the same pattern of decline as the SAP and the SPD, starting in 1983, with François Mitterrand's 180-degree turn from 'social rupture' to monetarist capitalism, which the French Communist Party (PCF) initially acquiesced to, in order to keep a few powerless ministerial posts. The French Socialist Party (PS) and PCF have now both ceased to exist as parties of any significance. Already by the mid-nineties, the main party of the French working class was the right wing Front National.

In economic terms, however, the (actually rather hollow) French egalitarian tradition has been more resilient than the German or the Swedish. To explain this falls outside the scope of this work, but it is not primarily due to welfare state redistribution, which is actually larger in the US than in France.[76] It is due to the considerably less unequal distribution of market income in France. Exceptions are glimmers of hope in the crevices of the iron laws of the status quo.

## Goodbye to the middle class

The ongoing inequality surge since 1980 has been driven from above, by the top 10 per cent, and above all by the top 1 per cent and smaller fractions of pharaonic wealth. The lower 90 per cent have not been impoverished, but they have been abandoned. This has given rise to a bitter journalistic and popular academic literature in the Global North, an interesting counterposition to the largely consultancy and development bank literature of middle class celebration both in and of the Global South.[77] It is a literature which should be taken seriously, as a significant, if special, approach to the rise of inequality.

In the current moment of liberal crisis and self-doubt, Iversen and Soskice present an upbeat homage to 'advanced capitalist democracies', with more deference to capitalism than to democracy, which is held responsible for the ongoing surge of inequality. They state that 'the essence of democracy is ...

the advancement of middle class interests.' The middle class, they argue, is aligned with capital via two key mechanisms. One is 'inclusion into the wealth stream' created by capital accumulation. They go on to say that, 'By far the most important path to such inclusion is education'. The other mechanism is the welfare state. 'The tax-and-transfer system ensures that these gains [of the knowledge economy] are shared with the middle classes.'[78]

It is precisely this 'inclusion' and 'sharing' between capitalists and the middle class that is currently denied and bitterly mourned by the prevailing literature in the Global North,[79] and found to be terminating by recent inequality research.[80] In the beginning, the neoliberal dispensation did favour middle class interests. The opening up of public services to private business has provided some gains for lucky segments of the middle class. Public funding of free private education places, through a voucher system as in Sweden today, has given middle-class parents a welcome chance to send their children to well-kept schools with few immigrant or working-class children. Corporate care has been less popular, and prone to public scandals, but is accepted by many as a familiar accompaniment to austerity and the scarcity of public provision. The selling of rented public housing to private landlords has increased the immobile wealth of the buyers, who can also cash in by moving to more peripheral housing.

But the increasing exclusion of the middle class from prime urban housing continues apace, and entry into increasingly important elite education is narrowing. Upward mobility is declining, and the income and wealth gap between the upper and lower classes is widening. Environmentalism is making ever deeper inroads into the educated middle class, explicitly putting planetary survival and ecological sustainability above the interests of capital.

As the median is the exact middle of a distribution, the ratio of top income to the median is a good measure of the distance between the upper and the middle classes. Proportionately, the leap of the Swedish upper class was the highest, more than trebling its distance from the middle. Meanwhile, the 1 per cent in the US has broken off contact not only with the national middle class but with all the other Western upper classes, and has retreated into a caste of its own. The French middle class has other good reasons to complain, as we shall soon see, but it has not been further economically decoupled from the rich.

In all parts of Europe, between 1980 and 2017 the incomes of the top 1 and top 10 per cent grew by more than those of the middle and upper-middle classes, whose incomes are between the median and the top 10 – the 'Middle 40', as French economists now call them. On the other hand, the middle classes have fared better than the bottom half of the population, except in the Nordic countries where their incomes have kept pace with one another. The distance between the Middle 40 and the upper class has widened more than the distance between

**Table 4.** Upper-Class Abandonment of the Middle Class: Ratio of Top 1 Per Cent to Median Income c. 1980–2016

| France[a] | from 10.5 to 9.6 |
|---|---|
| Germany[b] | from 7.2 to 11.25 |
| Sweden[c] | from 3.5 to 10.7 |
| UK[d] | from 3.3 to 9.9 |
| US[e] | from 11.2 to 25.8 |

Notes:
(a) Fiscal income, 1990–2014; (b) Post-tax, 1990–2016; (c) Disposable income, 1991–2016; (d) Fiscal household net income, 1980–2018; (e) Post-tax income, 1980–2014.

Sources: Sweden: Statistics Sweden, 'Disposable income per deciles 2018'. UK: calculation from Institute for Fiscal Studies data, equivalized with respect to the size and composition of the consumption unit, and from R. Joyce and X. Xu, 'Inequalities in the Twenty-First Century', Institute for Fiscal Studies, May 2019, Figure 3. The rest: World Inequality Database.

the Middle 40 and the half of the population that has been left behind. The difference between the two middle class distantiations, upward and downward, is largest in Eastern Europe and smallest in southern Europe.[81]

How the middle class is left behind by contemporary capitalism is also manifested in the remuneration of the CEOs of big corporations. In relation to the median pay of their own employees the median FTSE executive was paid 72 times more (in 2018), and 117 times more than the middle class (median) full-time worker in the UK. These figures constitute some moderation in comparison with the most recent preceding years.[82] But they sustain the new post-industrial class structuration. In 1980, an FTSE executive took home a pay package eighteen times larger than the average UK employee; in 1998, it was fifty-seven times bigger.[83]

The middle class is nowadays sometimes defined in aspirational terms. As the US Department of Commerce put it in a report to the Vice-Presidential Middle Class Task Force in 2010:

This report assumes that middle class families and those who wish to be middle class have certain common aspirations for themselves and their children. They strive for economic stability and therefore desire to own a home and to save for retirement. They want economic opportunities for their children and therefore want to provide them with a college education. Middle class families want to protect their own and their children's health. And they want enough income for each adult to have a car and for a family vacation each year.[84]

The post-1980 Great Inequality Surge has let the middle class down in these respects, most particularly in the US. The 'American Dream' has become a mirage. Whereas 95 per cent of boys born in 1940 earned more than their fathers at age 30, only 41 per cent of the 1984 birth cohort did. The main reason is not lower economic growth, but higher inequality.

If the children born in 1984 had been born into the income distribution of the US in 1940, 70 per cent of the decline in mobility would not have happened.[85]

In France, where total economic inequality has not increased, a drastic decline of mobility into the upper-middle class for the cohorts born after 1960 has been detected.[86] Because of the income polarization, the size of the middle income class – with incomes between 75 and 200 per cent of the median – has shrunk in the OECD area, and opportunities for entering into it have also narrowed. Seventy per cent of the generations born between 1943 and 1964 lived in middle-income households while in their twenties, but of the 'millennials' born after 1983, only 60 per cent are doing so.[87] By the age of forty, the proportion of those who are highly educated living among the top fifth of income-earners has declined, most notably in France, Spain, Finland, Ireland and Italy. Upward mobility into tertiary education has stalled in the OECD since 1975, and the risk of downward mobility (over a four-year period) from the middle class has increased substantially in the 2010s, most strongly in the UK.[88]

The OECD concludes in an overview of most of its member countries, not including the US, that 'Achieving a middle class lifestyle has ... become more difficult than in the past because of the strong rise in the prices of housing and other large middle-class consumption items [such as education and health care].'[89] In the US, tuition and fees at state universities and colleges rose by 230 per cent above inflation between 1980 and 2012.[90] In another time series, of family expenditure from 1970–2015, also adjusted for inflation, American family expenditure on housing increased by 57 per cent, on health insurance by 104 per cent, on college by 275 per cent, and on child care by 953 per cent, while men's earnings grew by 2 per cent.[91] Against fierce right-wing resistance, Biden's Middle Class Task Force and the Obama administration failed with respect to child care and college accessibility, as well as to health insurance, defined as a middle class attribute by the Department of Commerce.[92] In the UK, a 'generation rent' is succeeding the homeowners. In 2016, 46 per cent of people aged twenty-five to thirty-four were privately renting, up from 24 per cent in 2005–6.[93]

In the field of education, something much more brutal is befalling the American middle class. Its children and youngsters are being barred from an increasingly exclusive elite education system, spanning kindergartens to selective top universities, by the economically unmatchable investments upper class parents are making in order to prepare their offspring for plum positions in the labour market. The Yale Law Professor David Markovits has calculated that the costs of these investments in elite training, from pre-school to graduate school, above median (middle class) expenditure on education, have an equivalent value of an inheritance of $16.8 million. The result is that 'rich children now outscore middle-class children on the SAT by twice as much as middle-class children outscore children raised in poverty.'[94]

The metropolitan middle classes are also increasingly victims of spatial evictions and exclusions. For the US, the Stanford Center on Poverty and Inequality summarized the development from 1970 to 2009:

> One consequence of the rising income inequality has been a similar sharp increase in residential income segregation ... in 1970 two thirds of American families in large [>500,000 population] metropolitan areas lived in middle income neighbourhoods ... with median incomes between 80% and 125% of the median of their metropolitan area. By 2007 ... only 43% of families lived in such neighbourhoods. ... Middle-class neighbourhoods, like the middle class, are rapidly disappearing.[95]

A 2016 update from the same centre reported continued segregation. In 2012, 40 per cent lived in middle-class neighbourhoods, 30 per cent in high income or affluent areas (up from 16.5 per cent in 1970), and 30 per cent in poor or low-income neighbourhoods (19 per cent in 1970).[96] In London as a whole, median house prices quadrupled between 1996 and 2015, and in inner London they quintupled, while median wages fell by 10 per cent between 2008 and 2015.[97] The effect of this has been a decline of owner occupancy from 61 per cent in 2003–4 to 48 per cent in 2017–18, mainly due to a decline of houses bought by mortgage (the middle class way) from 39 to 27 per cent, lower than the proportion of private renters at 29 per cent.[98]

Stockholm is fully responding to the inegalitarian turn of Sweden[99] with rapidly increasing income segregation between 2001–11, to the surprise of a Dutch-directed research team with memories of the old Swedish welfare state. By 2011 Stockholm was roughly on par with London, its richest quintile more isolated, its lowest quintile less.[100]

Whoever governs these dismal democracies, it is certainly not the 'median voter' of economic theories of democracy.

## The professions undermined

The new capitalist political economy has left the middle class behind and outside. It is left behind in income and wealth. It has to live outside attractive inner cities, whether in London and New York or in Paris and Stockholm. It is left outside the best marketized health and old age care, because these have become too expensive. Its children risk being excluded from the best schools and universities and thereby from the best jobs, because of the expensive investments required, a process well advanced in the US and also now emerging in the UK. Over the whole OECD area, aspiring children are facing lower mobility opportunities.

Nor is this all. The very core of middle-class work is being undermined. Middle class work has had three major forms: self-employment, office work of some delegated authority, and the professions. Over the long run, the self-employed petty bourgeoisie, typically shopkeepers and their rural branch of farmers, have declined in numbers and importance. In the UK, though, there has been an increase of urban self-employed business-owners in this century. However, this growth is driven entirely by sole traders, most of whom are closer to the precariat than to the historical petty bourgeoisie, whose shops are drastically shrinking in number. Their mean annual income in 2015–16 was £21,000, a third of average employee income.[101]

Office workers and lower level managers are being subjected to what David Boyle has aptly called 'digital Taylorism'[102], before being dispensed with altogether, as has already befallen large numbers of post and bank clerks, for example. A white-collar office job is no longer a secure and relatively comfortable escape from the working class, but rather the main target of automation.

The third classical sector of a middle-class job was in the professions, occupations based on high and long education, handling particular kinds of knowledge, inaccessible to the public. They include ancient professions such as teaching, medicine, law, in many countries also the civil service, and the twentieth-century 'semi-professions' of nursing and social work, to name but two. They were for a long time respected by and seen as uninteresting to business and capital. In the German nineteenth- and early-twentieth century tradition they were often summed up as *Bildungsbürgertum* (the cultured bourgeoisie), which was more or less on par with the *Wirtschaftsbürgertum* (the economic bourgeoisie). Sociology has distinguished the professions from the business world, as oriented to the cultivation of knowledge and to public service, rather than to profit.

This middle-class professionalism is now under attack – lawyers largely exempted – and in the process of being destroyed. The attack comes from several angles, which may be summed up as invasion by managerialism. It involves a relative devaluation of specialist knowledge, a loss of respect for it. In practice this means first of all a subordination of professionals, teachers, researchers, physicians, nurses, engineers, and others, to administrative managers, in schools and universities, hospitals, and enterprises. The practice of professional knowledge is submitted to auditing, evaluations, and sanctions by managers, deriving from an institutionalized mistrust of professional autonomy and of professional ethics. Professional cognitive practice and ethics are subjected to pervasive cost-benefit calculations, often specially invented ones of internal quasi-markets, such as university administrations charging university departments for the use of university premises. These cost-benefit inventions are also part of a particularly heavy anti-professional attack under the banner of commerce.

The imposition of an ideal norm of commercialism – the instrumental opposite of the professional mindset of intrinsic values, of knowledge, of service to needs, of the impartiality of law and regulation – is operated both by private commercialization (of schools, hospitals, prisons, and so on) and by the so-called 'New Public Management' of tax-financed institutions. Internally the latter are supposed to work as firms on a quasi-market basis, buying and selling services to each other, and externally they are required to hire private firms to provide public services. In this way, education, health care and social care have become profitable areas for capital accumulation, attracting great interest from the 'economic bourgeoisie', knocking down the 'cultural bourgeoisie' on the latter's old terrain.

The middle-class professions should not be idealized, as they could very well become closed, conservative, complacent and inefficient, with repetitive routines. But this is not inherent in professionalism, and being a teacher, a doctor, a civil servant was once a great source of middle-class pride and self-confidence. That pride and self-confidence are now being trampled upon, and a managerial whip is overruling collegiality. A few succeed by escaping into an upper-middle class of managers and 'star' professionals, but for the rest, the present – and probably the future as well – consist of instability and a downward trajectory.

'Average is over', is the neoliberal epitaph for the middle class.

## V. Out of the Labyrinth

Democracy means rule of the people, not just some particular political game. Rule of the people was what people dreamed of, and fought for – people like the workers who produced the profits of capital, the (ex-)slaves who worked the settlers' occupied land, the Natives enserfed or chased away by the occupiers, the colonized who delivered the riches and glories of colonialism, the subaltern populations of the countries of Reactive Modernization, the women of all continents under the patriarchal yoke of unpaid labour obligations and lack of freedom. Fighting long and hard, the people who demanded equal rights for all to a decent life and equal possibilities of self-realization, were rarely strong enough to fully throw off the power and privileges of their masters. Almost always and everywhere, the lords of power and privilege retained their positions, and thereby their capacity to manoeuvre and to govern.

Modern democracy therefore arrived through labyrinthine trails, from various directions. Over the years, the impenetrable walls lining its meandering paths have only become higher and thicker. The spaces opened up by the democratic mass movements are currently shrinking, particularly in the economically most developed world. Nevertheless, radical democracy, in the sense of its heroic historical fighters, is not just a memory or an unclaimed inheritance. It is being reinvented by the popular egalitarian movements of recent years. International Occupy, the *Indignados* of Spain, the worldwide student Fridays for Future, the recent social protest movements in Chile, and in many other countries from Colombia to Algeria and Iraq, are practising direct, participatory, non-hierarchical, popular democracy. These movements, and many others, for all their limited sustainability, keep the historical idea of modern democracy alive and pulsating, despite the grey late-Liberal cynicism of democracy as a game for professional poker players.

What today is called or calling itself democracy is now in crisis, under challenge and suffering erosion in many parts of the world.[103] An argument of this book is that this crisis is due, above all, to the reneging by most existing democracies of their historical origins, in popular struggles for recognition, dignity and emancipatory social transformation. This is a legacy which we as citizens should lay claim to.

Today we need this universalist egalitarian legacy in order to be able to shape our future, in face of the flooding, the melting ice, the rising oceans, the drought and the bushfires already threatening it. The climate crisis we have been thrown into is a product of inequality and non-democracy putting the profit, growth and power of the few above the well-being of the many and their environment. According to Richard Heede at the US Climate Accountability Institute, the three biggest cumulative carbon emitters since the 1750s are Chevron, ExxonMobil and Saudi Aramco, producing 10 per cent of all carbon emissions in the planet over the last quarter milliennium.[104] At the Paris School of Economics, Lucas Chancel and Thomas Piketty have estimated that the top 10 per cent of the global emitters are responsible for 40 per cent of the emissions, and that since 2013 at least half of the inequality of carbon emissions is among classes within countries, and the other half stemming from inequality between countries.[105]

However, more important than responsibility for the past and the present is capacity for ensuring a liveable future for all of us. For this we need an egalitarian democratic world of trust and solidary efforts. We don't have it, and we are not very likely to get it in time for necessary action. But such a world has to be our compass direction, a world where profit, growth, power interests and luxury consumption are subordinated to the needs of the people and a sustainable environment; a world where coal miners and oil workers are ensured another decent way of earning a living, where populations of peripheries are no longer dependent on petrol or diesel to be socially connected; a world where everybody has equal rights to a decent life and to equal possibilities of sustainable self-realization – the same world that the pioneers of democracy dreamed of and fought for.

There is an intrinsic affinity between the student Fridays for Future movement initiated by Greta Thunberg to raise awareness of the climate emergency, and the egalitarian movement. Both are radical, democratic, universalistic, without fear or respect for existing powers. And their goals interconnect. In order to stop the destruction of the planet, humanity must become less unequal and more solidary. And human equality necessarily includes a liveable environment for everyone. Together, the climate movement and the egalitarian movement could become the game-changer of the twenty-first century. Therefore, expect many attempts to divide them.

## An egalitarian Enlightenment

The normative aversion to inequality reflects an elementary conception of human equality as well as a sensitivity to its violations, which have become characteristic of modern mainstream culture. We saw this above in the first section in which the worldwide perception of inequality is seen as a 'very big problem'. After the defeat of Nazism and of colonialism, the worldview of Übermenschen and *Untermenschen* (superhumans and subhumans) and of superior and inferior 'races' is no longer part of polite or respectable discourse, surviving only in delimited niches of human degradation and the extreme right-wing fringe, or mutating into new forms such as Islamophobia or neoliberal elitism.

In the wake of the 2008 financial crash, an international egalitarian Enlightenment has developed. Thomas Piketty, Emmanuel Saez, Gabriel Zucman and their associates at the New French School of Economics, are transforming the 'dismal science' of economics into bestselling illuminations of inequality.[106] Two former World Bank economists are weighing in as heavyweights, Nobel Laureate Joseph Stiglitz and Branko Milanović, a leading explorer of global inequality.[107] Another Nobel Laureate, Angus Deaton, is lending his name to a new inequality initiative by the far-from-radical Institute for Fiscal Studies in the UK.

Two of the three Nobel Laureates of 2019, Abhijit Banerjee and Esther Duflo, have characterized previous mainstream economics as 'bad', 'blinkered', and 'blind':

Bad economics underpinned the grand giveaways to the rich and the squeezing of welfare state programmes, sold the idea that the state is impotent and corrupt, and the poor are lazy ... Blinkered economics told us trade is good for everyone .... Blind economics missed the explosion in inequality all over the world, the increasing social fragmentation that came with it, and the impending environmental disaster, delaying action, perhaps irrevocably.[108]

Sociologists too are belatedly abandoning their geological notion of 'stratification', and are founding centres, institutes or programmes of inequality studies, from Helsinki to Johannesburg via the London School of Economics, Madison, Wisconsin, and Quito, as well as organizing international conferences on the subject in China, just to mention some personal experiences. Mainstream political science has begun to systematically study the inequality of political influence and power, as we noticed above, in works by Larry Bartels, Martin Gilens and others. Major interdisciplinary programmes of inequality studies have launched at top American universities, from Harvard to Stanford. The most prolific public writers on inequality in the UK are the epidemiologists Richard Wilkinson and Kate Pickett, and the Oxford geographer Danny Dorling.[109]

The intellectual current can be said to be turning when a senior professor at the Yale Law School publishes an indictment of meritocratic inequality, complete with a chapter on 'The Coming Class War'; when two professors of economics at Berkeley – one of them holding the exclusive marker of academic distinction, the Clark Medal – publish an investigation of recent US socio-economic history under the title, *The Triumph of Injustice*; and when the trailblazing author of the most popular recent coffee-table book on economics comes out in favour of 'really participatory and internationalist socialism' in his latest work, *Capital and Ideology*.[110]

Together with all the new multidisciplinary centres of inequality studies around the world, there is a global republic of egalitarian scholars emerging with something about it of the intellectual ferment of eighteenth-century philosophy, which prepared the road to the American and French Revolutions.

The main difference between the eighteenth-century Enlightenment and today's egalitarian Enlightenment is the contemporary strength of the Anti-Enlightenment,[111] for instance the plethora of lobbies, disinformation and dirty campaign specialists, the thick and loud mediascape of the status quo, and of the sheer diversity of organized particular interests with political agenda-shaping capacities. The old *anciens régimes* had nothing of this – although they had the dumb weight of unenlightened clergy – only some *post hoc* sharp intellectuals, like Joseph de Maistre, and a line of shrewd post-revolutionary politicians, like François Guizot, Louis Napoléon Bonaparte, Benjamin Disraeli and Otto von Bismarck.

In its 30 November 2019 issue, the *Economist* gathered

together a platoon of counter-Enlightenment economic arguments under the aggressive cover title 'Inequality Illusions'. In fact, the small print of the issue did not claim that the rise of inequality is an illusion, but mainly that the degree of inequality in the US is uncertain and contested, and, most importantly, that progressive Democrats should therefore abstain from raising taxes on the rich.[112] Such critiques centre on the complex estimates of the post-1980 rise of inequality in the US by Piketty, Saez, and Zucman. A non-economist had better abstain from any concrete comment, but their high standing, particularly in comparison with their critics, within an a priori rather unfriendly discipline, should give them the benefit of the doubt. My income analysis above, in particular of the abandonment of the middle class, is based on simple, undeniable data from public statistical sources.

## The feel of inequality

Inequality is an abstract concept, and as such more at home in publications of social science investigations or philosophical arguments than in kitchen table conversations. There is a bridge to be built between a predominant, elementary view of human equality in 'life, liberty, and the pursuit of happiness' and the inequality of life expectancy, income shares, and Gini coefficients.

What needs to be brought to the fore is the *feel* of inequality, its unfairness, its existential dimension. The hoarding of resources and of opportunities available to the few have serious human costs. While the number of billionaires is rising and wealth taxes falling or disappearing, in virtually all developed countries there are severe and growing crises of health care and old age care. Why? Because of a lack of resources. Public schools – in the more logical than British sense of state schools – are faltering; even their buildings are dilapidated. Why? Because of a lack of resources.

For the generations born after 1975, there are the shrinking opportunities for secure and satisfying jobs, for residence, not to speak of homeownership, in central areas, for liveable retirement pensions and in some countries for a system of higher education that is affordable for all and not just for the upper classes. There is the unfair division of labour, between on one side, executives and managers with hundreds of times the wages of ordinary workers, and golden parachutes if fired, and, on the other, the increasing number of workers in temporary employment, outsourced employment, and forced part-time employment, who may have to go to a foodbank to survive a spell of unemployment.

There is a sense of frustration and despair in experiencing all this unfairness, with profound effects on health, from depression – which affects about a fifth of US adolescents[113] – to 'deaths of despair' in the UK as well as in the US.[114] There is a sense of humiliation in not being able to provide your children with the means to fully participate in the lives of their friends with better-off parents. And a sense of injustice at taxation, for instance upon learning that Apple (which makes about 60 per cent profit on every iPhone 11 Pro), pays 1 per cent in tax (in Ireland), or that the 400 richest Americans pay lower taxes than their secretaries or workers.[115]

The lifestyles of the upper- and upper-middle classes are endangering the climate and environment for us all, with jet-setting, multiple cars, energy-demanding houses, luxury imports and so on. It has been estimated that the upper-middle class (the ninetieth percentile in the global income distribution in 2013) emits 4.9 times as much carbon dioxide as the world's middle (median) income group.[116]

Experiences of frustration, suffering and humiliation arising from inequalities are always local, concrete and specific, and will have to be spelled out as such. Moral outrage at tax dodging and climate destruction, for instance, are more general. Both are painful and important.

## *Is more equality possible?*

In our post-millenarian, post-utopian, and, more than any-thing, post-revolutionary era there is the decisive question of possibility, the last trench of conservatism. First, there are the denials of existence or significance, in this case of human social inequality. Then there are the debates about good or bad, of inequality as an incentive to the best and the bright-est, or as human suffering, of blocked life-chances, of painful stress, and of humiliation and frustration. In rational dis-course, egalitarians are winning the questions of what exists and of what is bad. However, the question of what is possible, socially, politically, economically, appears undecided.

Equality is a limit concept in the mathematical sense, an indeterminate term which we can approach more and more closely without reaching it or knowing if we have. Therefore the egalitarian question is, 'is less inequality, or more equal-ity, possible?'. There is a second, legitimate question in this context: 'Will more equality or less inequality be costly?'.

Few people today would seriously argue that less inequality is impossible. The world has seen substantial changes in the past, and is living with large inter-country differences in the present. The Netherlands and Sweden were about as unequal in 1916 as Brazil in 2015, measured by the national income appropriation of the richest 10 per cent. In 1960 the US top ten did not rake in much more than their Swedish counter-parts (32 per cent versus 31 before taxes).[117] The national Gini coefficients of income inequality in the world today range from 25 out of 100 in Slovenia to 65 out of 100 in South Africa.[118]

The costs of equalization are likely to be controversial, and decided only *post hoc*, after the event, if ever. The latest major conservative argument, by the Austro-American his-torian Walter Scheidel claims that substantial equalization is only possible with horrendous costs, state collapse, plague, natural disasters, mobilizations for large-scale industrial war, and Communist revolutions.[119] This is not correct. Not only is New Deal America a major exception to that rule, so is western Europe during the post-war decades – the period of the fastest economic growth in the region's history – as well as the Latin American experience of 2002–15.[120]

Relative inequality does not seem to matter much in rankings of national capitalist competitiveness. In the 2019 ranking of the World Economic Forum, four of the world's least unequal countries were among the top eleven most competitive ones (the Netherlands, Denmark, Finland and Sweden), alongside three of the most unequal developed economies: Hong Kong, Singapore and the US. One of the most unequal societies in Eastern Europe, Estonia, shares a top ranking with one of the least, Czechia.[121] In other words, loss of economic competitiveness or development potential is not a necessary cost of less inequality. The latter may as well be a boost. And the advantage of egalitarian competitiveness is, of course, that everybody, including generations growing up, can benefit from it.

### Winning the middle class

Politics is never reducible to sociology, but the latter may give useful hints of the limitations and potentials of the former. The dialectic of industrial capitalism, which Marx analyzed and predicted with impressive accuracy, is no longer operating in the Global North and has been stymied in the South. Post-industrial capitalism is no longer producing a growing, ever more concentrated working class. That process ended in the North in the period of 1965–80, when working-class social weight peaked. Advanced industrial capitalism with a strong labour movement was the social basis of the post-WWII equalization. The latter was also facilitated by industrial technology: the high productivity of the assembly line, for example, could sustain decent wages to non-specialized workers, if there were strong unions and a non-hostile political environment. Post-industrial capitalism, on the other hand, means constant inegalitarian headwind, making any progress more dependent on political mobilization and leadership.

In the Global South, manufacturing employment stalled in the 1990s, and industrial employment – including construction and mining – around 2010.[122] This is a major, if by no means fatal, handicap of equalization in Africa, Asia and Latin America.

Even if the sectors of the working class lost to the right could be won back, the labour movement is only a necessary component of egalitarian politics, no longer sufficient as its natural centre. Decisive to any successful egalitarian politics in the post-industrial era is a positive middle class policy of the left.

This is a very delicate and difficult issue, because an egalitarian middle class policy cannot abandon democracy's foundlings, nor the bottom half of the population to privatizations and income stagnation, nor the rights of employees against employers. It is the opposite of Blairism and the right-wing middle-class orientation, which has destroyed the French PS and the German SPD, the opposite of turning one's back on the people, of carousing with capital while representing an upper-middle class view of the world. The task is to convince the middle class – or substantial parts of it – of the advantages of equality and human solidarity over neopharaonic privileges and rewards for capital and its children.

The starting-point is that post-industrial, financial capitalism is abandoning and excluding the middle class. The upper class is abandoning the middle class economically, creating a 1 per cent versus the 99 per cent society. It is also increasingly excluding the latter, narrowing the paths of upward mobility, access to higher education as well as to higher incomes. In the US, which is a forerunner of this situation, the ultra-rich elite is shaping a set of exclusive life-courses of its own, from private pre-schools to elite universities to plum jobs in finance and aligned high-end careers. The middle class is increasingly excluded from the housing markets of Manhattan, inner London, Paris, and even Stockholm inside *tullarna* (the old customs gates).

Most of those making up the contemporary middle class in advanced capitalism are salaried employees, with rational employee interests in workplace rights, in work dignity, and in job security. Middle-class white-collar jobs are increasingly under attack from digitalized capital. Middle-class professions – with some exceptions like most lawyers and US physicians who are already privatized and commercialized – are being subverted and degraded by the intrusion of capitalist management into public service, once supposed to implement the state of law, to serve the public, and to maintain professional ethics and standards of knowledge.

There is at least a large sociological potential for a progressive, egalitarian middle class, and in a radical policy addressing it. The enthusiastic response by aspiring middle-class students to the Sanders and Corbyn campaigns of 2016 and 2017 indicates an opening. However, the acquiescence, so far, of the adult middle classes in their abandonment by the upper class, with their passive reception of the apocalyptic 'end of the middle class' literature, and their hegemonic media isolation from radical political currents, underlines the difficulties ahead. On the other hand, the huge, socially broad egalitarian demonstrations in Chile, started by students and soon followed by their parents, in the South American spring of 2019, also show the potential in the Global South.

### Political leadership

This is a necessary but unpredictable variable. However, the social conditions of politics are different today from those of the twentieth century, and in particular in the Global North. In the past, there were strong organizations, programmatically committed to egalitarian change. That is, the labour movement, in its different branches – Social Democratic, Communist, Socialist – and in some countries, like Scandinavia and parts of North America, also farmers' movements. Shadows of these organizations still exist, but they seem unlikely to provide any strategic leadership of social transformation.

What then? Appropriate leadership is unlikely to emerge from the top of organizational hierarchies; more probably it will be contingent and incremental. It will have to lead a heterogeneous set of egalitarian currents and protest movements into a viable democratic political project. In both respects there seems to be something to learn from studying Latin American experiences.

Latin American 'Populism', which should be studied primarily in its pre-power phases, has been a prime example of rallying wide social alliances around a radical, anti-oligarchic project. Its often disappointing spells of power are less relevant, because of the very different contexts of democracy in the South and the North.

To my knowledge, the most successful steering of a large but chaotic social movement into a viable political project was that of Argentinian Peronist politics in the early 2000s, issuing in the presidency of Néstor Kirchner – until then little known and rather peripheral within Peronism – duly constitutionally elected in May 2003 and continuing the egalitarian thrust of a movement which had caused the flight of Fernando de la Rúa a year and half earlier.

An egalitarian political leadership in the Global North of the early twenty-first century faces two large and difficult tasks, difficult in themselves and difficult, but necessary, to combine. One I have already touched upon, convincing and mobilizing a large sector of the middle class.

The party systems of the twentieth century have to change to provide space for an egalitarian middle-class politics. And they are changing, but so far, the changes have mainly been wrought by the right and to its advantage. Macronism and Trumpism, and the international rise of xenophobic parties, are telling examples. Changes have appeared on, and as a result of, the left as well, though so far with a more limited impact, due to stronger resistance – Syriza in Greece was ground down by the EU – or to internal ambiguity and division: the Five Star Movement in Italy, less so Podemos in Spain. As to when, or to what extent, new party systems will emerge and consolidate is still an open question. Thomas Piketty sees a new pattern emerging, between two poles, a highly educated, economically affluent 'Brahmin Left' and a 'Merchant Right', both divided, the former between egalitarians and marketeers, the latter between Nativists and straight business.[123] There is a satirical connotation in the Brahmin epithet, and the consequences of an 'egalitarian' high caste government are likely to be as contradictory as Nehru's India or British Blairism. Some other pole will be necessary, anti-oligarchic, listening to and winning the confidence of both the middle class and the populace, which the Latin American populist leaders did, in their way.

Egalitarian politics in the twenty-first century will depend crucially on its capacity to rally the middle class. Part of the middle class is already on the left, for ideological and/or environmental reasons, but the decisive thing is winning the economic argument.

The other big task, also decisive, is re-gaining the trust and the support of the bottom half of the population, the losers of neoliberal globalization. The fact that a large proportion of working class and poor people, the historical and the rational base of egalitarian politics, has been captured by the right has redrawn the political landscape of both Europe and the US. It was decisively facilitated by the self-indulgence of what

Piketty calls the 'Brahmin Left'. Egalitarian political leadership must mean, first of all, listening to, and taking seriously the worries, complaints and demands of the working-class and of the poor. A criterion of egalitarianism is respect for these people, as well as for all other people.

An egalitarian left cannot adopt a Brahmin contempt for or ignorance of poor people's worries about free trade, immigration, and the concentration of employment and public services in affluent or densely populated areas. First of all, it has to listen, before preaching. Then it has to provide some constructive proposals – and listen to the response.

In Britain, Brexit is unlikely to become a benefit to the English working class and precariat. But these people voted for it, and as democratic citizens they expected the referendum result to be respected. The Labour Brahmins argued, de facto, forget the northern popular majorities, we want to remain in the EU. Corbyn tried to keep the party together with a complicated compromise, which also included a refusal to listen to the historical base of Labour on a matter of vital concern to it. The popular verdict was delivered on 12 December 2019.[124]

Listening to, discussing with, and convincing the working class Tory Brexiters, the poor or ordinary voters of the Front National, of the Italian Lega, of Trump, of the Sweden Democrats, and their equivalents in other countries is the second decisive task of an egalitarian political leadership. It will require a natural popular political style as well as a listening ear and persuasive principled arguments. For the moment no such leadership is in sight, but that is par for the course in this unpredictable century.

## Social change and disruptive democracy

Social transformation is not 'normalcy', and the fact that business-as-usual is unlikely to bring radical social change is only to be expected. Most of the time, elections in capitalist countries are rigged against egalitarians, by the professionals of the political game, with their personal data collections and menus of diversionary issues to catapult into prominence; by the media houses of the status quo; by campaign donors; sometimes by gerrymandering; in some places by intimidation. The exact outcomes may not be decided in advance, but they tend to stay within the confines of conventional politics. Opportunities for social change are structurally minimized, and increasingly so with the professionalization of campaigning. Openings are never to be excluded, however, and electoral nihilism is a dead end.

Radical change has indeed happened in the past. But over the last century we have seen a shift in egalitarianism from organized and programmatic to latent. The four major democratic movements of the twentieth century, the working class movement, the feminist, the Civil Rights movement (Black and indigenous), and the anti-colonial were all programmatically egalitarian, in one formulation or other. As democratic movements they were all successful, and when they got into power they had an egalitarian agenda.

Now, previous equalization is being rolled back, and there are few strong political parties or movements with an egalitarian programme. Popular egalitarianism has not disappeared, as we saw from the global Pew research at the beginning of this chapter, but it has become more latent than organized, with sporadic outbursts rather than a continuous accumulation of strength.

Under what conditions could popular egalitarianism come into open play? 'We must ask ourselves,' argued the British political scientist Colin Crouch sixteen years ago in the shadow of Tony Blair, 'without a massive escalation of truly disruptive actions ... will anything reverse the profits calculation of global capital enough to bring its representatives to the negotiating table ... to force an end to ... growing extremes of wealth and poverty ...?'[125]

Ordinary people matter little in actually existing democracies. That is the sad conclusion of contemporary political science. And that is why many ordinary people are mistrustful of politicians and the political system, creating crises of liberal democracies and generating spectres of 'populism'. As we have shown above, this is not the democracy ordinary people historically fought for and sometimes died for. Another democracy should be possible, a disruptive democracy. Rule of the people, democracy, has to be recognized as depending on popular movements, popular protests, popular riots, as well as on political parties, elections, and representative institutions.

In our times of disorganized, latent egalitarianism, the huge mass movement in Chile in October and November 2019, whatever its outcome, is one probable future. That is, latency exploding unpredictably, by contingent triggers. Another scenario, also contingent and unpredictable, is a disruption of the existing party system, opening up a window of electoral opportunity to more equality.

'Disruptive innovation' is one of the most fashionable business ideas of the twenty-first century. An egalitarian and environmentally sustainable society would be a large-scale disruptive innovation out of post-industrial capitalism. If we ever do manage to come near it, one way or the other it will only happen through a disruptive democracy.

## VI. The World after Corona: Vistas of 1945 and 1932

The Corona pandemic has caused enormous social disruption, and continues to do so at the time of writing. It may be seen as foreboding the coming climate change disasters of this century. It is already, before its end, the largest calamity of humankind since World War II. As such it is likely to become a watershed in modern human history. As far as can be understood at this point, the pandemic involves two very different sets of experiences, from which very different post-pandemic responses will follow. One is social, socio-economic and socio-medical, the other is geopolitical.

The social set of experiences involves at least three aspects. First, the high and bitter, often lethal, human costs. While the virus itself made no class distinctions, its contagion and its effects on human bodies were structured by social inequality. By 1 April 81 per cent of the global workforce lived in countries with required or recommended workplace closures.[126] The locked-down population ranged from the upper classes – those who helicoptered themselves out of quarantine, as in Santiago de Chile, or who expanded their e-businesses while firing workers complaining about unsafe working conditions, like Jeff Bezos of Amazon – to the tens of millions of rightsless migrant workers, locked out of their meagre daily living and locked into overcrowded slum housing, as in India, or into dormitories in the Gulf states and Singapore. An international divide opened up between an upper and upper middle class that could work and direct their business moves from the safety and comfort of their homes, and the ordinary working people who have lost their livelihoods, or have had to risk their health and even their lives feeding the affluent salariat or caring for their elderly parents. In the US, by mid April a good half of the workforce was laid off. Forty to fifty per cent of the upper middle class could work from home, compared to only 3 per cent of the bottom fifth.[127]

The second social experience of the crisis has been the deadly failure of private health and old age care business and management: millions of workers left without health insurance; a large shortage of medical equipment, from protective gear to ventilators and test-kits; deficient low-cost management of nursing homes, exposing frail elderly to infection by untrained, unprotected temporary staff. The governor of New York, Andrew Cuomo, found it 'unbelievable' that the US could not produce the medical equipment it needed, and instead had to buy from China.[128] In frustration, the Spanish government took control of the private hospital and nursing home sector, while the British (Conservative) governmental press briefings on the epidemic featured a permanent 'Protect the NHS' (the public health service) slogan.

Thirdly, there was a sudden rediscovery, recognition, and re-awakening of the state. The former leader of German Social Democracy, Sigmar Gabriel, exclaimed 'We have underestimated the state for thirty years'.[129] The size of state support interventions promised, by April 2020, are often unexpectedly impressive, amounting to almost half of the GDP of Italy, and a good 9 per cent of output in the US, although so far no more than 0.9 per cent of India's low GDP.[130]

Not just the Left but also people of the political middle-of-the-road are likely to draw the conclusion from these experiences that inegalitarian neoliberalism is no longer acceptable. The Depression put an end to pre-Keynesian liberalism; COVID-19 is most likely to bury post-Keynesian neoliberalism.

This may be called the vista of 1945, after the hopes and demands for a better world that arose not only from the horrors of the war but also from the hunger and unemployment endured under the upper-class misers of the 1930s. Such was certainly the opinion of the British electorate in 1945, and it finds a contemporary echo in the *Financial Times* editorial of 3 April 2020 cited in the Preface. However, in 1945, almost all the forces of evil and inequality were seen as having been defeated, smashed even. That is unlikely to be the case by the end of the coronavirus crisis.

So far the COVID-19 pandemic looks less lethal than the Spanish flu of 1918–20 or the fourteenth century plague. But it has a claim to be the largest synchronised crisis in human history, and is unique for taking place in a world wholly dominated by nation-states. The contagion has set the stage for renewed nation-state competition and for power games by big nation-state actors. It is bound to have significant geopolitical effects.

From the start the nation-state politics of the pandemic were driven by an 'us first' approach, including an almost complete break-up of the supposedly sacrosanct four freedoms of EU, with border closures and export bans of relevant medical equipment, even if already ordered and paid for, and the US outbidding French and German equipment imports from China on the tarmac of airports in France and Thailand.[131] This might be interpreted as a political panic which gradually quieted down, but a resurrected North-South divide within the EU has persisted.

On a global scale, the pandemic produced at least two important geopolitical experiences. One is the superior performance in coping with the virus by East Asia, the other is the increasingly belligerent response to this by the US and its followers in the world.

At this stage, always a necessary qualification, the superior performance of East Asia, the heirs to the ancient Sinic civilization and its deep culture of collective organization, is rationally, empirically undeniable. The number of virus deaths is the best available indicator – far from perfect, since registration criteria are not fully standardized, but countries like France and China have upgraded their data for comparability.

On 1 July at 11.41 GMT, East Asian COVID-19 deaths per million population amounted to 8 in Japan, 6 in South Korea, 3 in China, 0.9 in Hong Kong, 0.3 in Taiwan and 0 in Vietnam. Among Western powers the death toll so far was 644 in the UK, 606 in Spain, 575 in Italy, 457 in France, 393 in USA, 228 in Canada, and 108 in Germany. The Western average is 430, the East Asian is 3, a West-East mortality ratio of 143:1.[132]

It seems to be impossible for Western media, academics, and politicians to accept that East Asia is outperforming the West. This is not the proper place to try to explain why this is so – factors may range from SARS 2003 epidemic experience to public culture and state capacity – but the broad political spectrum of the countries should be noticed. The original national political response – from dismissal to panic – was succeeded by an aggressive US anti-China campaign. It was clearly first of all a domestic electoral tactic by the Trump regime, but one which rapidly gained a resonance among the politicians, pundits and academics of Natoland and its Australian offshoot, a close US ally from the wars of Korea and Vietnam.

According to this narrative, the virus and the Western failure to cope with it are caused by China, and more specifically the Chinese Communist Party. Therefore China has to be punished.

This vista is no longer that of 1945, but rather 1932, when the forces of hatred and violence were still on the march. Violent, aggressive nationalism is on the rise, which might turn an existing trade war into a conflict of bombs and bullets. The Depression led to radical social reform in Scandinavia and the US, briefly also in France. But it also led to Fascism, and to World War II. Fascism is no longer on the agenda, but war is being culturally prepared by the mounting barrage of China- and Russia-bashing.

The danger is hardly a deliberate US attack on China, but rather an escalation of insults and provocations getting out of control.

For the world this is a bleak prospect, and not only because of the human costs of a US-China war. A successful anti-China campaign would kill the climate movement, and make a planetary response to a planetary challenge impossible. In order to survive, the climate change movement will have to become at the same time a movement for peaceful coexistence between the different regimes of the world. The social inequality of humankind is even more inter-national than intra-national. Nationalist aggression is aggression against humanity. Egalitarian disruptive democracy will have to disrupt the mobilizations for exclusion, hatred, and war.

# 2

# The Rule of Capital and the
# Rise of Democracy

The relationship between advanced capitalism and democracy contains two paradoxes – one Marxist and one bourgeois. Any serious Marxist analysis has to confront the following question: How has it come about that, in the major and most advanced capitalist countries, a tiny minority class – the bourgeoisie – rules by means of democratic forms? The bitter experiences of Fascism and Stalinism, and the enduring legacy of the latter, have taught the firmest revolutionary opponents of capitalism that bourgeois democracy cannot be dismissed as a mere sham. Does contemporary reality then not vitiate Marxist class analysis? Present-day capitalist democracy is no less paradoxical from a bourgeois point of view. In the nineteenth and early twentieth centuries, as both political practice and constitutional debate clearly demonstrate, prevailing bourgeois opinion held that democracy and capitalism (or private property) were incompatible. Even such a broad-minded liberal as John Stuart Mill remained a considered opponent of democracy for this very reason. He advocated the introduction of plural votes for entrepreneurs, merchants and bankers, as well as their foremen-lieutenants and professional hangers-on, in order to forestall proletarian 'class legislation'.[1] In modern times, however, since at least the outbreak of the Cold War, bourgeois ideologists have maintained that *only* capitalism is compatible with democracy. What has happened? Is this perhaps just a *post hoc* rationalization of a historical accident?

Before going any further, we should make absolutely clear what we understand by 'democracy'. The term is here used to denote a form of state with all the following characteristics. It has (1) a representative government elected by (2) an electorate consisting of the entire adult population, (3) whose votes carry equal weight, and (4) who are allowed to vote for any opinion without intimidation by the state apparatus. Such a state is a *bourgeois* democracy in so far as the state apparatus has a bourgeois class composition and the state power operates in such a way as to maintain and promote capitalist relations of production and the class character of the state apparatus.[2]

Popular representation and free and equal suffrage are the crucial variables with their necessary prerequisites, freedoms of opinion, speech, assembly, press, and organization.[3]

Although this chapter presents only a few preliminary reflections, and is by no means a definitive account, it will clearly have need of a representative sample of cases. Future studies will have to draw upon the experience of all existing capitalist countries, but at this stage, it is the advanced ones that are most important. One of the least arbitrary ways of choosing a sample is simply to take the members of the OECD, which seems to be the broadest and most significant organization of the core capitalist states. At present its members include: Australia, Austria, Belgium, Canada, Denmark, Finland, France, the German Federal Republic, Greece, Iceland, Ireland, Italy, Japan, Luxemburg, the Netherlands, New Zealand, Norway, Portugal, Spain, Sweden, Switzerland, Turkey, the United Kingdom and the United States. There are other important capitalist states, such as Brazil, India and Iran, but the OECD countries seem to constitute the central nucleus of capitalism. At the time of writing (March 1977) none of these is a fully-fledged dictatorship, although Turkey and Spain do not yet have stabilized democracies. The real heart of the OECD appears to be the seventeen major capital-exporting states – excluding, that is, Greece, Iceland, Ireland, Luxemburg,

Portugal, Spain and Turkey – which make up its Trade and Development Committee. It is these seventeen, then, that I shall take as my representative sample.

I am concerned here with the process whereby democracy became the established form of bourgeois rule under advanced capitalism. My task, then, will be first to locate its appearance in time, and secondly to situate it in social and political space. For these purposes, neither the correlational techniques of the sociologists nor the institutional sequences of Stein Rokkan are adequate. What is required is rather a comparative historical overview which seeks to identify general patterns while remaining sensitive to the peculiarities of each particular case.

## I. The Tasks of Democratization

Since even formal democracy cannot be said to exist either completely or not at all, it is sometimes very difficult to establish an exact date for the achievement of democracy. But if we are able to isolate the democratic values of my four defining variables, it should then be possible to discover when they were attained in the various countries under consideration.

The democratic principle of popular representation implies the existence of either a republic or a parliamentary monarchy. The predominant regime of nineteenth-century Europe – a constitutional monarchy in which the cabinet had no clear-cut responsibility to Parliament – cannot then be held to fulfil the conditions of democracy. Nor was this true of non-sovereign states like pre-1918 Finland or British colonies before they reached independent or dominion status. For representative government clearly implies popular sovereignty. In my sample of seventeen countries, the process of attainment of representative government stretched over a period of two centuries: from the mid-eighteenth century, when a parliamentary cabinet was consolidated in Britain, to 1952, when US occupation of

Japan was terminated and the 1947 democratic constitution took effect as the basis of a sovereign state.

The introduction of universal suffrage required the dismantling of a number of restrictions, typically based on criteria of tax-payment and income. Where two legislative bodies existed side by side, as was often the case, these qualifications would normally be considerably higher for one of the chambers. Of a certain importance were also limitations based on standards of literacy (as in Italy until the new electoral law of 1911, and in the southern states of the USA well into the twentieth century) or on membership of a particular sex (invariably the female), race (Blacks in the USA, Chinese in the USA and Canada), or (parts of) a given class (wage-labourers with a household of their own in Denmark and Britain). Further minor restrictions, excluding people on relief, for example, were not insignificant in the early stages of democratization, but we shall not deal with them here.

The achievement of equal suffrage also involved the abolition of plural voting – which survived in Britain until 1948, although it was of little import after 1918 – and the elimination or emasculation of a privileged upper House. More intractable has been the practice of gerrymandering and disproportionate allocation of seats. With the exception of Norway, where under the 1814 constitution the reverse tendency operated, almost all the countries we are considering have had, and to a varying extent retain a clear over-representation of rural voters (presumably more conservative). However, this does not seem to have been a very significant electoral factor since the other variables began to correspond to the conditions of democracy, and we have left it out of the present analysis.[4]

When we talk of a free vote, we are of course referring only to norms supported by the force of law: to freedom from intervention by the state apparatus in the electoral process; and to the right to present candidates of any persuasion, and vote for whichever is preferred. In the past, Napoleon III and Giovanni

Giolitti in pre-1914 Italy became masters of the management of elections by sections of the state apparatus – from the Ministry of the Interior down to local prefects and even postmen.[5] In modern times, the intimidation of Blacks by the regional and local state apparatus in the United States provides one major illustration of these methods, but the typical pattern of restricting democracy has rather been the banning of opposition parties.

In *What Does the Ruling Class Do When It Rules?*, I argue that a bourgeois government is, in a minimal, non-evaluative sense, always a regime of national representation. This provides us with two dimensions within which to delimit the characteristic space occupied by a particular regime. Which nation is represented? How is it represented? The nation as expressed in the institutional arrangements of the polity – the *pays légal* – may quite simply comprise the entire adult population. But it may also embrace some more than others – by means of plural votes, delineation of constituencies, and so on. Or such nations may even exclude from political participation sections of the population who have little or no property or who belong to a certain race, sex or set of opinions.

The mode of representation may be exclusively elective, but it may also be self-proclaimed. A regime may be based, for instance, on the claim of a Leader or an apparatus of the state (usually the army) to represent and incarnate the will or interests of the nation. Between these polar extremes lies another, historically important mode of representation which combines the two. The non-parliamentary constitutional monarchies of nineteenth-century Europe provide us with the best examples of such regimes. They combined a non-elective, proclaimed representation of the nation by the king – the King of the French, etc. – with elected legislatures.

Combining the variables of national representation and of an electoral system, we get four basic types of modern nation-state regimes:

1. Liberal exclusivism, with an elected representative government and effective but restricted suffrage.
2. Authoritarian exclusivism, with a non-elective government claiming national representation and an effective but restrictive parliamentary suffrage.
3. Dictatorship, non-elective national representation with non-effective suffrage.
4. Democracy, elective government with effective universal suffrage.

## II. The Historical Establishment of Democracy

Now that we have defined the criteria of bourgeois democracy, we should attempt to locate the period of establishment in the seventeen countries. In order to gain some bearings for the causal analysis that follows, and to explicate the datings in Table 5 (some of which may appear far from self-evident), we should survey the most decisive events in each different country.

*Australia.* The Australian colonies became a federal state with the ambiguous sovereignty status of a dominion in 1901. Already in the 1890s, Lib-Lab coalitions in individual colonies had started introducing the universal and equal white suffrage which was to form the basis of the federal franchise of 1903. The qualifications were blatantly racist, and indeed section 25 of the constitution still explicitly allows for discrimination in state electoral laws. However, even in the decade before the dominion status was achieved', the principal racist thrust had been directed at the exclusion of prospective non-white immigrants (by means of skillfully contrived European-language tests which, after British protests, had been imported from the Natal[6]) and at the expulsion of Chinese and Pacific immigrants already there. Behind the walls of this exclusive continent,

**Table 5.** Year of Establishment of Democracy

| Country | First attainment of democracy | Male democracy (if prior) | Reversal (excl. foreign occupation) | Beginning of present day democracy |
|---|---|---|---|---|
| Australia | (1903) | | | |
| Austria | 1918 | | 1934 | 1955 |
| Belgium | 1948 | 1919 | | |
| Canada | (1920) | | (1931) | (1945) |
| Denmark | 1915 | | | |
| Finland | (1919) | | 1930 | 1944 |
| France | 1946 | 1884 | | |
| Germany | 1919 | | 1933 (1956) | 1949 (1968) |
| Italy | 1946 | (1919) | [1922] | 1946 |
| Japan | 1952 | | | |
| Netherlands | 1919 | 1917 | | |
| New Zealand | 1907 | | | |
| Norway | 1915 | 1898 | | |
| Sweden | 1918 | | | |
| Switzerland | 1971 | c. 1880 | ([1940]) | ([1944]) |
| UK | 1928 | 1918 | | |
| US | c. 1970 | | | |

Note: Brackets denote qualifications, square brackets a process of reversal or re-establishment of male democracy.

Sources: Basic electoral data and constitutional contexts are from D. Sternberger, B. Vogel and D. Nohlen (eds), *Die Wahl der Parlamente*, Berlin 1969, and H. Tingsten, *Demokratiens seger och kris*, Stockholm 1930. The political dynamics are gathered from a number of national historical sources, specific points of which are referenced in the country surveys shown in these tables.

racism had a limited significance – although it was only in 1962 that the tiny aboriginal population was finally granted the federal vote.[7]

*Austria.* In 1907, following the revolutionary events in Russia and massive working-class demonstrations in the country itself, virtually universal and equal male suffrage was introduced in elections to the second chamber in the Austrian part of the Habsburg dual monarchy. Only after the fall of the Habsburgs in 1918 were full universal suffrage and a parliamentary government established. The new democratic republic was the work of a tripartite coalition in which the Social Democrats were initially the central force. But Austrian politics soon came to be dominated by the overwhelmingly farmer-based Christian Socials Party who in 1934 installed a reactionary dictatorship, itself to be swallowed up four years later by German Fascism. After the defeat of the Nazis and the end of allied occupation, Austria started out on its present democratic road.

*Belgium.* The struggle for universal and equal suffrage was the focus of massive working-class strikes in 1886, 1888, 1891, 1893, 1902 and 1913, all of which were defeated, sometimes with severe repression.[8] Finally, at the end of the First World War, the ruling Catholic Party accepted universal suffrage, after twenty-five years of a system of heavily weighted male voting in which middle-aged heads of propertied families disposed of three votes. The post-war national coalition government called elections on the basis of equal male suffrage, and the resultant Parliament amended the constitution accordingly.[9] Responsibility for the very restricted female franchise lay mainly with the Liberals and Social Democrats, who feared that women voters would tend to support the Catholics.[10] Full universal suffrage was not adopted until 1948. A male democratic franchise for elections to the Senate was also introduced in 1919, but workers and small entrepreneurs were still not among the twenty-one categories eligible to stand as candidates.[11]

*Canada.* Property qualifications continued for a long time to restrict the franchise, persisting in the provinces of Québec and Prince Edward Island until after the Second World War. But in the struggle for military conscription – much detested in Québec in particular – a Conservative government considerably extended the franchise in 1917 and in 1920 universal white suffrage was introduced for federal elections. However, racially discriminatory electoral legislation was permitted to the provinces and once more authorized by franchise acts of the 1930s. British Columbia and Saskatchewan continued to make use of this possibility until the end of the Second World War. As regards political exclusion, the small Communist Party was raided in 1931 and its leaders imprisoned. Officially prohibited in 1940, the party was able to reappear after Stalingrad as the Labour-Progressive Party, but its single elected MP was soon deprived of his seat under a mysterious espionage charge.[12]

*Denmark.* In 1849, under the triple impact of a succession to the throne, nationalist agitation focusing on the unclear status of the king's German-Danish dukedoms, and the March Days (the more peaceful equivalent of the French February Revolution), Denmark moved from an absolutist regime to a bicameral constitutional monarchy in which the lower chamber was elected by equal and virtually universal male suffrage. Cabinet responsibility to the farmer-controlled second chamber was secured in 1901 after a protracted struggle with an upper house dominated by the landowning aristocracy in alliance with the big urban bourgeoisie. A left-liberal government, based on the small farmers and urban petty bourgeoisie and actively supported by the Social Democrats, then proposed a democratic, bicameral constitution including women's right to vote. The last attempts of right-wing landowners to maintain significant conservative guarantees – attempts which had the sympathies of the big farmers' Left party[13] – faded away in the national union that was established on the outbreak of the First World War. However, the democratic constitution adopted in 1915 included a very high electoral age limit of twenty-nine years.

*Finland.* The general strike and mass workers' demonstrations of 1905 led the Finnish Estates, meeting not far from

the St Petersburg Soviet, to transform themselves into a uni-
cameral legislature elected by universal suffrage – a solution
subsequently accepted by the Tsars. Women received the vote
both because the labour movement demanded it and because
the Conservatives thought they could count on their electoral
support.[14] But Finland remained part of the Russian Empire,
and the executive council – the Senate – did not take on the
responsibility of a Parliament.[15] After the civil war of 1918, the
victorious Whites set out to install a non-parliamentary constitutional monarchy under a German prince. However, the fall
of the German Empire later in the year frustrated these plans,
and in 1919 a bourgeois republic was proclaimed. Although
the Communist Party remained illegal, it was able to operate
through a front party until a strong fascist-type movement
based on the farmers put an end to this in 1930. Only in 1944,
after the defeats of its German ally, did the Finnish government
join the full democracies and lift the ban on the Communists.

*France.* The democratic constitution of 1793 was the first in
the world to include universal male suffrage, but it was never
put into practice and was formally revoked after Thermidor.
The similar provisions adopted after the February Revolution
were in turn severely restricted by the bourgeois Parliament
in 1850, and, although they were restored by Napoleon III in
1852, it was in the absence of free elections and parliamentary government. Military defeat of the Second Empire and
stalemate between rival royalist factions laid the basis for the
republican constitution of 1875. Thus, from the year 1884,
when the republican advance secured an alteration of the
privileged upper chamber, France may be described as a male
democracy. The Communist Party was banned on the outbreak
of the Second World War and, after the defeat of 1940, a non-
democratic pro-German satellite regime was installed until the
Liberation. The new constitution of 1946 went on to extend
the franchise to all adult women. Throughout the twentieth

century, the history of the French republics has been punc-
tuated by revisions of constituency boundaries and electoral
procedures introduced with the aim of putting the opposition
at a disadvantage.[16]

*Germany*. The popular conquest in 1848–9 of effectively
universal and equal male suffrage was swiftly reversed by pro-
capitalist royal reaction. Later, Bismarck introduced a male
franchise for Reich elections as a means towards national
unification and as a weapon against the bourgeois liberals.
The establishment of a regime of parliamentary democracy,
in which the reformist Social Democrats played the leading
role, came about only after the military defeat of Wilhelmine
Germany. Present-day West German democracy may be said to
date from the end of the Allied occupation that followed the
fall of the Third Reich. However, the relatively small Communist Party was banned in 1956 and only allowed to reappear
under a new name in 1968.

*Italy*. After unification, Italy had a very narrow suffrage until
1912, when the Liberal Giolitti introduced the male vote as
part of his campaign for support of the Libyan war. However,
the state apparatus remained active in 'management' of the
elections right up to 1919,[17] and a conservative Senate blocked
a positive proposal for female suffrage. Although the government's parliamentary base lay in the Chamber of Deputies,
a significant role was thus still played by the Senate, whose
members were appointed by the king according to a number
of criteria that included possession of considerable wealth and
a distinguished career rank. Even the existing elements of male
democracy were, of course, quickly eradicated by Fascism and
a fully democratic constitution was only adopted in 1946.

*Japan*. The Japan of the Meiji Restoration came to take the
German Reich as its model, and the 1890 Constitution was

written with the help of German jurists. Universal male suffrage was introduced in 1925 following the post-war years of popular struggle. Although no genuine system of representative government and political freedom ensued, parties and elections were permitted until the establishment of a military dictatorship under Imperial cover in the late 1930s. Japan may be regarded as a bourgeois democracy since she recovered her sovereignty in 1952 on the basis of a constitution drawn up by the US occupation authorities six years previously.[18]

*The Netherlands.* The 1795 Dutch revolution put up a Constituent Assembly with a wide franchise, from which the Orangist monarchists were excluded. Democratic advance was stopped by Napoleonic and post-Napoleonic domestic counter-revolutions. By the end of the nineteenth century, male citizens had to demonstrate 'signs of capability and prosperity' to be able to vote. The Liberals and the religious parties were divided on democracy, and the only consistently democratic force, the Social Democratic Labour Party, was rather weak. The national emergency of the First World War, which the Netherlands could stay out of, changed the situation. Male universal suffrage was finally incorporated in a wide-ranging deal between all parties, whereby the religious ones received full state support for confessional schools. The deal was eventually implemented under the auspices of a Liberal government in the 1917 climate of national unity, but it accorded with the recommendations of a pre-war commission.[19] Owing to the opposition of religious politicians, female suffrage was delayed until 1919. Further constitutional amendments of 1922 restricted the already much weakened powers of the monarch.

*New Zealand.* After three decades of parliamentary government and a franchise based on property qualifications, a sort of male democracy was instituted in 1889 by a rather conservative government in the wake of left-Liberal and Labour agitation. Four years later, female voting rights were introduced by a Labour-backed Liberal administration, largely under the pressure of prohibitionists anticipating widespread women's support.[20] The Maoris had been given four seats in the House in 1867. Thus the principal democratic changes had already been implemented before the country acquired dominion status in 1907.

*Norway.* The struggle against the union with Sweden was led by the urban intelligentsia and petty bourgeoisie, who managed to rally the farmers around them in a liberal Left party. However, when it formed a parliamentary government in 1884, the Left came out in opposition to universal suffrage. Labour movement agitation in the 1890s finally persuaded the liberals to yield in the hope of uniting the people for the final battle with the Swedish monarchy.[21] Practically the whole male population gained the vote in 1898, followed by women fifteen years later.

*Sweden.* A slow political development, discontinuing an eighteenth-century parliamentarism of four Estates led to a modern parliamentary government only in 1905, a national coalition facing the Norwegian secession. Fifteen years of social-democratic and liberal campaigning were necessary before a Conservative government finally granted men wide and equal voting rights to the Second Chamber of the Diet in 1907. Propertied interests were safeguarded by a First Chamber with equal powers, indirectly elected through municipal plural voting according to income. The scale ranged from 0 to 40 votes, considerable progress, from 0 to 5000 previously. A Liberal-Social Democratic government bill in the spring of 1918 proposing equal rights and the inclusion of women was voted down by the First Chamber. In October 1918 the Right still said no, but in early November the German Reich was crumbling and a revolution broke out. In Sweden the king and representative business leaders of finance and industry started to pressure the rightwing parties, the landowners, the agrarian bourgeoisie, the old state establishment, and sectors of the urban petty bourgeoisie. Five days after the revolution in Berlin, the government presented anew its electoral reform, slightly more extensive. This time there was no resistance.[22]

*Switzerland*. The traditional oligarchies of the Swiss cantons fell to the male democracy of artisans, peasants and intellectual petty bourgeois in the 1830s and 1840s, in several cases after armed uprisings. Although the national civil war of 1847 was fought over the issue of national unification versus provincial clericalism rather than over democratic rights, the two struggles were in practice different moments of the same revolution. The federal constitution of 1850 prescribed male democracy, but it can hardly be said to have institutionalized it, for the following decade was filled with cantonal rebellions and counter-rebellions.[23] It is in fact extremely difficult to date precisely the consummation of the process. A host of ingenious devices of intimidation and manipulation, as well as significant legal exclusion clauses (relating to bankruptcy, tax payment, and so on) continued to be employed for several decades by the cantonal state apparatuses. In Berne in 1874, for example, as many as 25 per cent of the total male population were effectively excluded from the franchise.[24] The establishment of male democracy was included in the Constitution of 1874, but may perhaps be located more accurately about the year 1879, when a proper electoral register was drawn up for the first time. Out of accommodation to Nazism, the Communist Party was banned in 1940. But when the fortunes of war turned, so did those of Swiss male democracy – in 1944 the party was allowed to reform as the Party of Labour. Women's rights, however, found no place in the predominant conceptions of democracy and, even after the male political establishment acquiesced to female suffrage in the 1950s, sexist referenda delayed its attainment until 1971.

*United Kingdom.* In the middle of the eighteenth century, Britain became, alongside Sweden, the earliest parliamentary monarchy. The birthplace of industrial capitalism, Britain witnessed also the first democratic working-class mass movement, as well as the first effective crushing of such a movement in the 1840s. The male franchise was considerably extended in 1867 and 1884, but it was only during the war, in 1918, that more or less equal and universal suffrage was legislated by a Liberal government. Provisions for a more restricted female vote, which had been successfully opposed before the war, were also approved. Equal women's suffrage was granted by the Conservatives in 1928 after the first minority Labour government had failed to get it accepted. Relatively insignificant instances of plural voting rights were finally abolished by Labour in 1948.

*United States.* The American road to democracy has been a tortuous one indeed. Starting in Connecticut in 1855 and Massachusetts in 1857, the trend which had appeared in the first half of the century towards removing the original property qualifications was for a time reversed by the introduction of literacy tests to exclude the new poor Irish immigrants.[25] The Fifteenth Amendment enfranchised Blacks in the northern states, but it took another hundred years for it to take effect in the South. There, both Blacks and poor Whites were intentionally barred from voting by poll taxes and manipulative literacy requirements, as well as by semi-official intimidation. It was not simply racist ideology that lay behind these practices: the aim, which was successful for more than half a century, was also to establish a one-party regime of the upper bourgeoisie.[26] In the North, the significance of literacy tests was soon eroded, but the fresh requirement of advance registration in person on the electoral list proved more effective in discouraging the lower strata from political participation. Thus in Massachusetts 4 per cent of adult male citizens were excluded from voting in the 1908 presidential elections because of literacy qualifications, whereas a further 13 per cent failed to register.[27] The combined effect of northern registration obstacles and the southern one-party regime was a reduction of participation in presidential elections from 75–80 per cent in the period 1876–1900 to an average of 60 per cent in the twentieth century.[28]

In the northern states, White and Black women obtained the vote together just after the First World War. But it was only in the late 1960s, after violently resisted civil rights struggles in the South and ghetto rebellions in the North, that the federal government began to enforce the Fifteenth Amendment in the South. The Amendment had been passed shortly before the centenary of the republic, but it was only just in time for the bicentennial celebrations that the United States fully qualified as a bourgeois democracy.

## III. Patterns of Democratization

In the history of democratization, two features are striking by their absence. Firstly, the fact that none of the great bourgeois revolutions actually established bourgeois democracy. It is not only of the early Dutch and English revolutions that this is true: the democratic constitution produced by the French Revolution remained a dead letter from beginning to end of its brief existence. The July Revolution did not even manage to draft one, although it did stimulate the development of a male democratic movement in Switzerland. The international popular upsurge of 1848 was rapidly stifled by a feudal-dynastic reaction – and also by the bourgeoisie itself. For example, in 1850 the Second French Republic deprived 2.8 million adult males of the vote by the introduction of lengthy residence qualifications.[29] Similarly, the Danish bourgeois National Liberals eagerly assisted in clipping the wings of the popular chamber in the 1860s. The American Republic was established by White propertied gentlemen, and the only Blacks enduringly enfranchised by the Civil War were male northerners. Unified Italy took over the extremely narrow franchise of the Kingdom of Sardinia. And when, despite the misgivings of the bourgeois liberals, Bismarck introduced universal male suffrage in Reich elections, a regime of parliamentary democracy was neither the object nor the outcome of the measure.

The second striking absence in the history of bourgeois democracy is that of a steady, peaceful process accompanying the development of wealth, literacy and urbanization. On the eve of the First World War, only three peripheral capitalist states could have been characterized as democracies: Australia and New Zealand (where rampant racism was able to turn outwards rather than inwards) and Norway. If we disregard sexism and include male democracies, then two more examples could be cited: France and Switzerland. The latter had recently passed through two civil wars – in 1847 and 1874 – whereas the former had experienced a number of revolutions and counter-revolutions, as well as the military defeat of the Second Empire, which became the starting-point of the democratic republic. The long-standing British parliamentary regime had still not enfranchised the whole male working class, and was only slowly beginning to relax after its repression of the first democratic mass movement in history. In the United States, the process of democratization had suffered two reverses: one in the North, directed against new illiterate immigrants, the other turned against Blacks and the poor White opposition of the South. In Italy, prefects and the *mazzieri* (thugs armed with clubs) of the liberal premier Giolitti still largely controlled the elections. In other countries likewise, big landowners and their *kulak* and bourgeois allies retained the power of privilege.

In order to provide an overview of the temporalities involved in the process of democratization, we must now chart the political pattern of these seventeen countries at given points in time (Table 6). Countries will be included only after they have gained independence, with the exception of Norway, which, prior to 1905, was the minor partner in a royal union with Sweden rather than an integral part of it. Italy and Germany appear only after national unification; Austria after the Hungarian *Ausgleich* of 1867 and the end of absolutism; and Japan after the Meiji Restoration. Until these changes, they all clearly belonged to a different universe of regimes. (The Habsburg Empire, for example, was never a bourgeois state proper.)

### Democracies by military defeat

After the First World War the number of democracies increased from three to ten (with some qualification in the cases of Canada and Finland), and that of male ones from five to fourteen. By 1939, however, the number had fallen to eight and eleven, respectively. The big boom of democracy came in the aftermath of the Second World War, with only Swiss sexism and US racism holding out until the 1970s. The conclusion would appear to be that bourgeois democracy is largely a martial accomplishment.

The victors of both world wars made ample use of democratic rhetoric, and none more so than the least democratic of capitalist states – the United States of America. But no serious historian seems to have suggested that the wars were caused by a struggle for or against bourgeois democracy, or that Germany and her allies lost because they did not possess democratic regimes. Moreover, the crucial historical role of foreign wars provides strong support for the thesis that bourgeois democracy is largely contingent to the developed rule of capital. If this is true, then the fragility of bourgeois democracy in Latin America may be partially attributed to

**Table 6.** Bourgeois Regimes at Selected Points in Time

| | Democracy | Liberal exclusivism | Authoritarian exclusivism | Dictatorship |
|---|---|---|---|---|
| **The 1850s** | | | | |
| | | Belgium | Norway | (France)[a] |
| | | Denmark | Sweden | |
| | | Netherlands | | |
| | | (Switzerland) | | |
| | | UK | | |
| | | US | | |
| **1914** | | | | |
| | Australia | Belgium | Austria | |
| | New Zealand | Canada | Germany | |
| | Norway | Denmark | Japan France | |
| | | Italy | | |
| | | Netherlands | | |
| | | Sweden | | |
| | | Switzerland | | |
| | | UK | | |
| | | US | | |
| **1920** | | | | |
| | Australia | Belgium | Japan | |
| | Austria | France | | |
| | (Canada) | Italy | | |
| | Denmark | Switzerland | | |
| | (Finland) | UK | | |
| | Germany | US | | |
| | Netherlands | | | |
| | New Zealand | | | |
| | Norway | | | |
| | Sweden | | | |
| **1939** | | | | |
| | Australia | Belgium | | Austria[b] |
| | (Canada) | Finland | | Germany |
| | Denmark | France | | Italy |
| | Netherlands | Switzerland | | Japan |
| | New Zealand | US | | |
| | Norway | | | |
| | Sweden | | | |
| | UK | | | |
| **The 1950s** | | | | |
| | Australia | Switzerland | | |
| | Austria | US | | |
| | Belgium | | | |
| | Canada | | | |
| | Denmark | | | |
| | Finland | | | |
| | West Germany | | | |
| | Italy | | | |
| | Japan | | | |
| | Netherlands | | | |
| | New Zealand | | | |
| | Norway | | | |
| | Sweden | | | |
| | UK | | | |

Notes: (a) The Bonapartist regime of the French Second Empire is difficult to place in a simple scheme of ideal types: it differed both from the traditional nineteenth-century constitutional monarchies and from the twentieth-century dictatorships.
(b) 1934–1938, then incorporated into Nazi Germany.

the fact that it was never drawn into the mass slaughter of two world wars.

It may be the case, however, that the accidental origin of bourgeois democracy is itself an accident. For even if they scarcely figured among the major capitalist powers, three countries did have democratic regimes prior to the First World War, and they have retained them ever since (disregarding the German occupation of Norway between 1940 and 1945). It would appear, then, that world wars are at least not indispensable conditions of bourgeois democracy. Perhaps there were even internal processes of democratization at work, which only accidentally burst forth after the world wars. At all events, we had better avoid the terrain of correlational analysis, so beloved by many contemporary political scientists, and examine the causal forces in operation. We shall also have to indulge in some counterfactual speculation about the possible course of political history if the world wars had not occurred or had ended differently.

Let us count the four states which jumped on and off the democratic stage as each representing two instances. We then have a total of nineteen cases instead of seventeen. In nine of these, a regime of bourgeois democracy resulted from the military defeat of a non-democratic government (Austria, Finland, Germany, twice each, and Italy, Japan and Sweden, once). In two of these (Finland 1918–19, Sweden 1918), it was the fall of a foreign regime – Wilhelmine Germany and, before that, the Romanov Empire – which had an indirect effect on the process of democratization. In the Finnish example, it seems perfectly clear from the development of constitutional negotiations after the White victory in the civil war that, had it not been for the establishment of a democratic republic in Germany, a constitutional but non-parliamentary monarchy would have been proclaimed. Half a year after the collapse of the Reich, it was still an open question whether a democratic republic would be accepted by the interim head of state, General Mannerheim, and by the forces of the Right.[30] But there was no equivalent to the solid Hungarian aristocracy and Mannerheim was not to become the Finnish Horthy.

In the case of Sweden, counter-factual argumentation is rather more hazardous. In the late autumn of 1918, the country was in a situation of near-revolutionary turmoil. Left-wing forces, striving for a socialist revolution and greatly inspired by the Russian October, constituted a clear minority of the labour movement, whereas the popular pressure for bourgeois democracy was very strong. Nevertheless, the Right was entrenched in the non-democratic First Chamber and could count on both the support of the landowners, prosperous farmers and mighty wood and steel combines of pre-industrial origin and on the loyalty of the officer corps and police. It was undoubtedly the king's fear for his throne, among other considerations, that finally persuaded the politicians of the Right to relinquish the privileges to which they had clung so stubbornly. It seems almost certain that the process of democratization would have been postponed for some time further if Germany had emerged victorious. What would have happened had there been no war at all is more difficult to assess. The Swedish Right had grown stronger and more aggressive as the storm clouds gathered over Europe after 1912, and it is unlikely that it would have accepted a democratic regime by late 1918 without the fall of its much admired Wilhelmine Reich.

Similarly, the course that would have been taken by the Habsburg and Hohenzollern Empires in a period of peaceful development is impossible to state with any assurance. However, they would hardly have blossomed into parliamentary democracies by 1919. In the event of military victory, too, the *Junker* nobility and the masters of big capital would hardly have given up their privileges or retreated before the internal forces of democracy.

A World War II victory of Germany, Italy, and Japan would obviously have precluded their democratization for an indefinite time.

In conclusion, we can say that in eight cases out of nineteen (or in five out of seventeen) the outcome of the world wars was causally decisive in the instalment of bourgeois democracy – without excluding the possibility of a later democratization – and that in one more (Sweden) it determined the timing of the process. To these six democracies whose origins lie in military defeat, we may add the case of France. For the precondition of the male democratic republic that developed was the collapse of Napoleon III's Empire in the Franco-Prussian war.

In only four countries was the process of democratization totally unrelated to foreign war: Australia and New Zealand, Norway and Switzerland. However, in six of the thirteen other democracies in my sample, war seems to have had an indirect effect or to have been of only secondary significance in their development. It served to influence existing governments and parties in the direction of democracy rather than to break up old forces and bring forth new ones. Indeed, it would be more correct to consider this type of effect under a more general heading, covering additional important steps in the process. Thus, from the war democracies proper – the democracies by defeat – we should go on to examine the democracies of national mobilization.

## National-mobilization democracies

National mobilization has been related to the development of democracy in two basic ways. On the one hand, measures of democratization have been introduced as a *means* towards the end of national mobilization; on the other, they have been produced as *effects* of the process of integration (military, economic and ideological) expressed in popular mobilization for the national effort. The two clearest examples of the former are Giolitti's franchise reform in Italy and the Canadian War Times Elections Act of 1917 – both parts of the political preparations for war. The second relationship is illustrated by the establishment of male democracy in Belgium, the Dutch reforms of 1917–19, the Danish Right's acceptance of democracy in 1915, the British Reform Act of 1918, and the introduction of female suffrage in the United States in 1919 (perhaps also in France and Belgium after the Second World War). In all these cases, a process of democratization already underway was speeded up and facilitated by a wartime *union sacrée*. This effect of mobilization was very well expressed by King Albert I of Belgium, speaking to Parliament on 22 November 1918 upon his return to Brussels: 'Equality of suffering and endurance has created equal rights in the broadening of public aspirations. The government will propose that the two chambers dismantle the old barriers in a patriotic agreement and initiate national consultation on the basis of equal suffrage for all men who have reached the age required for the exercise of civil rights.'[31]

In other cases as well, national mobilization has played an important role in extension of the suffrage. Bismarck, for example, wrote in his memoirs: 'the acceptance of general suffrage was a weapon in the struggle against Austria and the rest of the foreign powers, a weapon in the struggle for national unity'. But his intention was that only candidates for the propertied classes should be allowed to compete for the votes of the masses.[32] In the same spirit, one of the reasons why the Austrian emperor conceded general male suffrage in elections to the Second Chamber in 1907 was his hope that this would neutralize tendencies towards disintegration of the dynastic empire into its component nations.[33] Similarly, the Danish bourgeoisie was led to accept a general franchise as an instrument of its struggle to replace the king's Germanic dukedoms of Schleswig, Holstein and Lauenburg by a national, non-dynastic frontier on the Eider river. In Norway, the need to rally the people behind the fight against the union with Sweden appears to have been one of the main reasons for the (liberal)

Left Party's acceptance, in 1898, of the labour movement's strong demands for male voting rights. Semi-revolutionary working-class demonstrations formed the background to the extension of the Finnish franchise in 1906 as part of the struggle against the Russian Tsar.

Mobilization for national liberation and foreign war has thus, alongside military defeat, been one of the most important causes of the development of bourgeois democracy. But it is more difficult to ascertain how decisive this role has been. It has been a crucial determinant of the timing of democratization and one of the reasons for the coincidence of war and democracy. But would the internal processes have come to a halt without these external threats? It seems likely that in the Netherlands and, above all, Denmark where a parliamentary majority had already tabled proposals shortly before the outbreak of the First World War, the tempo of events would not have been much slower in the absence of national wartime integration. In Norway, however, the establishment of democracy would almost certainly have been delayed for some time had it not been for the unresolved conflict with Sweden. In Canada, where property and poll tax restrictions persisted at a provincial level long after the introduction of a federal franchise in 1920, the war seems to have affected the process in a decisive manner. But for the war, the militant Belgian Catholic Right would hardly have surrendered by 1919, and it would also have taken longer for women to gain the vote in Belgium, France, the Netherlands and, possibly, the United States.

In Britain, reform was already at quite an advanced stage. The franchise had been considerably extended in 1867 and then in 1884; free elections had been guaranteed; the House of Lords had been rendered virtually powerless just before the war; and a bill abolishing plural voting had been published. Nevertheless, no decision had been taken on general male suffrage, not to speak of universal voting rights, and although the process would doubtless have continued even under peaceful conditions, it is likely to have taken a longer time to reach completion.

Concluding, then, we can say that national mobilization in the face of external threat has been a most important factor in the history of bourgeois democratization. In two countries – Denmark and, perhaps the Netherlands – it was of only secondary significance, determining the more or less consensual manner in which the critical steps were taken. In four cases – Belgium, Britain, Canada, Norway – it speeded up the achievement of male democracy to a varying, uncertain, but probably considerable extent. In five countries – Belgium, Britain, France, the Netherlands, the US – it brought female enfranchisement nearer. (We should also remember that the voting rights of Blacks in the American South were first enforced during the Vietnam war, quite possibly as a result of the government's concern with a crumbling home front marked by Black rebellion, student movements and opposition to the war.) But in none of the cases under consideration is it possible to state that national mobilization was a necessary condition of democracy.

## Internal-development democracies

There are only three countries where democracy has been produced by internal developments alone: Australia, New Zealand and Switzerland. But we should also consider those cases where such processes were of primarily temporalizing significance, namely, Denmark, the Netherlands, the UK, and the United States. In France, the establishment of democracy rested upon a uniquely complex fusion of external defeat and internal evolution. Finally, since the four examples of national mobilization referred to above – Belgium, Britain, Canada, Norway – also exhibited major internal tendencies, we shall have to take them into account under this heading.

The working-class and the labour movement were major constants of the development of democracy. The Second International went down in ignominious disarray in 1914, but its contribution to the development of bourgeois democracy was certainly not insubstantial. Indeed, democracy may be said to have been its principal historical accomplishment. However, although the labour movement was the only consistent democratic force on the arena, it was nowhere strong enough to achieve democracy on its own, without the aid of victorious foreign armies, domestic allies more powerful than itself, or splits in the ranks of the enemy.

Two internal factors seem to have been of the most immediate strategic importance: the independent strength of the agrarian petty and small bourgeois farmers, and divisions within the ruling-class (or power) bloc.

It is hardly surprising that the tiny privileged minority constituted by the mercantile and industrial bourgeoisie and the feudal and capitalist landowners should have been almost invariably hostile to democracy – hence the exclusivist outcome of the bourgeois revolutions. By contrast, the urban *artisanat* and petty bourgeoisie generally tended in a democratic direction and provided the striking force of both the Jacobins and the 1848 revolutions. But, as these examples also show, they were too weak to hold out against feudal and bourgeois reaction. The peasantry, however, constituted an absolutely decisive force in the still largely agrarian capitalist countries of the nineteenth and early twentieth centuries. Now 'peasantry' is, of course, far too undifferentiated a notion. The landless peasants were, on the whole, still too oppressed to say or do very much, although in Finland the crofters very soon became an important part of the labour movement and later played a heroic role in the civil war. The ones who really counted were the small and medium landholding farmers, including patriarchal self-subsistence households, the agrarian petty bourgeoisie and the small and medium agrarian bourgeoisie (those using hired labour).

The strength of these agrarian classes – and the degree of their independence from the landowning aristocracy and urban big capital – were crucial factors in the development of democracy. They were most powerful in the Swiss cantons, which had withstood the Habsburg Empire for centuries, and in the settler communities of Australia, New Zealand, the northern United States and Western Canada. The isolated mercantile patriciates of Berne and Zurich were as little able to resist these forces as the pastoralist squattocracy of the antipodes and its allies amongst recently formed urban capitalists. The beginning of male democracy preceded the rise of the workers' movement in both Switzerland and the northern United States. In Australia and New Zealand, trade-unionist labour politicians occupied an important place in the democratic coalitions, but posed no socialist threat to capital. In the large and bitter strikes of the early 1890s, sheep and shipping capital inflicted, with the help of the state, serious defeats on the seamen's and shearer's unions. (It is worth remembering, however, that Australia had quite a strongly organized agricultural proletariat as early as the 1880s.) In Canada, by contrast, the small settlers were no match for the wealthy mercantile bourgeoisie on the Saint Lawrence river, the Tory squires of Ontario and the traditionalist French community of Québec, closely shepherded by the Catholic hierarchy.

Pre-industrial poverty and semi-colonial dependence, which had for centuries kept Finland and Norway on the periphery of European society, almost completely prevented the formation of a native aristocracy. All that was able to develop was a thin and largely urban crust of Danicized nobles and patricians in Norway, and an only slightly stronger stratum of Swedish aristocrats in Finland. These were far too weak to support an aristocratic autocracy of the kind that was installed in Horthy's Hungary after the fall of Wilhelmine Germany and the victory of domestic counter-revolution. Although the French aristocracy returned after Waterloo to take up its old positions in state and church, it had been decisively broken by the Great Revolution. Thus, by the middle of the century, the free landed peasantry was strong enough to provide the popular support for Louis Napoleon's shrewd institutionalization of universal male suffrage.

The Danish landowners were much stronger than their Swedish counterparts. Nevertheless, the internal process of democratization developed much earlier in Denmark, largely because of the differential impact of the crisis that hit central European agriculture in the second half of the century. The victory of protectionism in Sweden in the late 1880s split the old Yeoman Party and forged an alliance, rather similar to the one in Germany, between landowners and prosperous farmers linked to classical heavy industry (wood and iron); modern engineering industry, like *Elektrochemie* in Germany, tended towards a more liberal direction.[34] In Denmark and the Netherlands, however, farmers turned to dairy production, building up a strong co-operative movement in which they lost the interests they had shared with the big landowners. By overplaying its hand at a time when its economic hold over the countryside was being undermined, the Danish aristocracy soon made it impossible to reach a viable agreement with an agrarian bourgeoisie that was far from enthusiastic for democracy, but was clearly opposite to the landowner Right.

It is impossible to disentangle here the reasons why the Belgian farmers so docilely followed the leadership of the Catholic Party (a formation which, though *encadré* by the lower clergy, was effectively controlled by the aristocracy). They disposed of a fairly important organization – the *Boerenbond* – with which to defend their economic interests, but they remained socially and politically isolated in their Flemish countryside from the industrialized and secularized French-speaking parts of the country. This lack of an active political role also characterized the economically powerful Dutch farmers. Although I am not able fully to assess the political significance of the phenomenon, it is clear that agrarian class relations in Belgium and the Netherlands present marked differences from the pattern prevalent in Scandinavia, France and other countries of continental Western Europe. The fact that a large proportion of farms were rented suggests that a certain degree of personal dependence has survived the introduction of intensive commodity production. Unfortunately, the latest figures available to me are for the years 1929–30, when 57 per cent of Belgian and 46 per cent of Dutch farms were rented, compared with 20 per cent in France and Sweden and (in 1949) 4 per cent in Denmark.[35]

However, as the case of Britain shows most clearly, the existence of a vigorous agrarian small and petty bourgeoisie is by no means a necessary condition of democratization. In fact, Britain, like France, although in a rather different way, provides an excellent example of the second critical internal factor mentioned above – a divided ruling class. There have been at least two ways in which, under certain circumstances, splits have come to play an important determining role. As long as there is no serious threat from below, divisions can lead to intense vying for popular support; and provided that there exists a degree of underlying unity (if only because of previous disastrous experiences of violent conflict), they may help to promote institutional procedures securing peaceful coexistence and opposition.

The waves reaching Britain from revolutionary France and the first steps of the labour movement were all effectively crushed by a unified ruling class. However, the early and immature bourgeois revolution resulted in the establishment, by the nineteenth century, of a deeply rooted parliamentary pattern based on competition within the ruling class between landed and urban capital. When the counter-revolutionary panic subsided, and especially when popular agitation re-emerged in more cautious forms, this rivalry developed into a struggle for broader mass support. The important extension of the franchise by the Conservative Disraeli government in 1867 offers a brilliant illustration of this feature. Parliament and the Tory Party itself were caught in an unstable balance of power, while outside popular pressure for electoral reform was mounting. After a series of complicated manoeuvres, in which Disraeli's main objective was to out-trump his Liberal rivals and to secure the leading position within his own party, the government-sponsored bill was finally carried by a parliamentary majority. In mid-nineteenth century Britain, a Conservative politician could possess such enormous class self-confidence that a handful of parliamentary radicals, playing the competitive game of the ruling class, managed shrewdly and inostensibly to extend the suffrage further than the government had intended. The key thing for Disraeli was to beat the Liberals, who opposed the bill from the right.[36]

Developments in France constituted a more violent variation on the same theme. The much more radical bourgeois revolution had both seriously estranged the urban bourgeoisie from the landowning aristocracy and definitively emancipated the peasantry. The latter made Louis Napoleon president in 1848, while the nobles prevented the consolidation of bourgeois reaction in the period from 1849 to 1851. After the military defeat of the Second Empire and the crushing of the Paris Commune, divisions within the royalist camp of reaction produced a stalemate, which led to the formation of the non-democratic Third Republic. Torn by internal dissensions, this bloc fairly rapidly succumbed to the democratic republican forces of the small bourgeoisie and petty bourgeoisie.

In the late nineteenth and early twentieth centuries, extremely complex divisions within the Dutch ruling class also facilitated the process of democratization. The Liberal Party split into three. The Calvinist Anti- Revolutionary Party, which supported a male household franchise while opposing both individual and property-based suffrage as expressions of the 'rule of Mammon', suffered a split when a faction more closely tied to aristocratic and big farmer interests broke away to form the Christian Historical Union. Some democratic elements even appeared within the generally conservative Catholic Party. The resultant combination of bourgeois democracy with lay acceptance of state-supported religious schools – a compromise which was reached in 1917 – and reinforced religious party control of large sectors of 'the little people' (kleine luyden) proved an effective barrier to the emergence of a unified working class capable of using bourgeois democracy to advance its own interests.[37]

The importance of ruling-class divisions operating within a solid underlying framework of unity is further demonstrated by the arduous and protracted process of democratization in the United States. The Fifteenth Amendment, forbidding electoral discrimination on the grounds of race, was not the result of the Civil War. Nor was it seriously intended to enfranchise Blacks in the South, since the vitally important task was to reunite the northern and southern fractions of the bourgeoisie. 'The effect of the amendment', wrote its sponsor, the Republican senator of Nevada, William Stewart, 'has been what I supposed it would be, to secure for the negro in the northern states his right to vote without intimidation.'[38] The amendment was proposed by the Republicans after their relatively poor performance in the 1868 elections, in order to ensure majorities in the North and in the union. Meanwhile, the Democratic plantocracy was allowed to entrench itself in the South.

It is of course difficult to sum up in a few lines the complex history of the forces of democracy in the American South. However, if we compare the situation of the 1960s with that of a century before, two striking differences emerge. In the 1860s the Black ex-slaves had no independent, organized force with which to conduct opposition or a policy of alliances – and democracy has never been handed down from above. A century later, a militant Black movement had established itself in the industrialized and urbanized areas of the South, and, by the third quarter of the twentieth century, the old rural bourgeoisie of the deep South had become marginal to the national ruling-class bloc. It is this that explains the ability of the federal state apparatus to move in to enforce democratic rights without fear of provoking serious splits of the bourgeoisie. In 1965, half of the states still had literacy requirements for voting, but their effectiveness had been eroded even before the absorption of new immigrant workers into the system by the bosses of the urban political machines.

Any attempt to chart the dominant patterns in each country carries serious risks of oversimplification. Table 7 should therefore be seen only as a rough indication of the forces that contributed directly to the achievement of bourgeois democracy. The only fairly clear-cut cases are Belgium, the war democracies proper, and the three countries – Australia, New Zealand and Switzerland – where democratization was a wholly internal process. A number of qualifications should be made concerning other countries. Thus, to a significant extent, Norway owes her democracy to its autonomous agrarian popular classes. Federal Canadian democracy emerged both as means and effect of national mobilization; and national integration also played an important role in Denmark and Britain. Military defeat was an important factor in France, while in the northern United States, democracy was largely an achievement

**Table 7.** Patterns of Democratization

| Democracies by defeat | | Democracies by national mobilization | | Democracies by internal development | |
|---|---|---|---|---|---|
| *Direct* | *Indirect* | *As means* | *As effect* | *Petty bourgeois independence* | *Ruling-class division* |
| Australia | Sweden | Canada | Belgium | Australia | France |
| Finland | | Norway | Netherlands | Denmark | UK |
| Germany | | | | New Zealand | US |
| Italy | | | | Switzerland | |
| Japan | | | | | |

of farmers and of the small and petty bourgeoisie. Nor does the table give full justice to the Dutch small and petty bourgeoisie, which was rather more to the fore than its Belgian counterpart. Finally, it should be stressed that underlying all these patterns was a common, consistent force: the working class. In a certain sense, different patterns may be said to express the different allies necessary for the success of the working-class struggle for democracy.

## IV. Capitalism and Democracy: Inherent Tendencies

Bourgeois democracy has been attained by such diverse and tortuous routes that any straightforward derivation from the basic characteristics of capitalism would be impossible, or at best seriously misleading. Nevertheless, the facts that democracy in the sense defined above did not appear anywhere prior to capitalism; that some capitalist countries have experienced a purely internal development of democracy; and that all major advanced bourgeois states are today democracies – these naturally call for some elucidation of the tendencies inherent within capitalism. These may provisionally be grouped according to their effect upon two central features of bourgeois democracy: (a) inclusion of the masses in *part* of the political process, (b) under conditions of representative government and electoral competition.

We may list six factors bearing upon the outcome of socio-political tendencies inherent in capitalism.

1.Bourgeois democracy has always succeeded mass struggles of varying degrees of violence and protractedness. The first inherent tendency, then, will be found in *the conditions favouring popular struggle*. Legal emancipation of labour and the creation of a free labour market, industrialization, concentration of capital are all intrinsic tendencies which simultaneously lay the basis for a working-class movement of a strength and stability unachievable by the exploited classes of pre-capitalist modes of production. In accordance with Marx's analysis of the growing contradictions of capitalism, the working class is, *ceteris paribus*, strengthened by the advance and development of capitalism. This explains the traditional sociological correlations of democracy with wealth, literacy and urbanization – factors which bear upon the relationship of forces in the class struggle. And, as we have already seen, the labour movement has itself played a crucial role in the struggle for democracy.

2. However, we also remarked that in general the working class has not won a share in the political process in the heat of battle. On the contrary, it has been more common for the bourgeoisie to make concessions after a period of successful resistance to reform. Apparently, working-class participation must in some sense be to the bourgeoisie's advantage. Although in Germany and Austria in 1918 and 1945 (possibly also in Belgium and Sweden in 1918) and in Italy in 1945 the alternative to bourgeois democracy was an attempted socialist revolution, actual defence against proletarian revolution does not seem to have been a directly determining factor. In all these cases, it was not the insurrectionary proletariat but foreign armies that overthrew the existing regimes, whereupon the old internal democratic forces at last got the upper hand.[39] Of greater importance was the specifically capitalist art of industrialized warfare. The First World War was fought both with massive conscript armies and with whole civilian populations mobilized for military production. For this effort even the German Reich admitted the Social Democrats into the governmental machinery; against this background, too, the suffrage was extended in Belgium, Canada, Britain and the United States.

3. National unification and liberation have everywhere been seen by the bourgeoisie as a strategic necessity for the development and protection of trade and industry and the breaking of feudal dynastic power. And for these aims it has often found it invaluable to enlist popular support. The extension of suffrage in Denmark, Germany, Norway, Finland and Italy (for the imperialist Libyan expedition) formed part of a process of national unification.

4. Feverish development of the productive forces is another feature peculiar to the capitalist mode of exploitation. One of the main reasons why nineteenth- and early twentieth-century liberals denied the compatibility of democracy with private property was their dread that popular legislatures and municipal bodies would greatly increase taxation. However, they were disregarding the elasticity and expansive capacity of capitalism. Higher levels of taxation have liquidated neither private property nor capital accumulation. Rises in productivity make possible a simultaneous increase of both rates of exploitation and real incomes of the exploited masses.[40] This is, of course, not in itself conducive to democracy. But it is relevant in so far as it provides the bourgeoisie with an unprecedentedly wide room for manoeuvre in dealing with the exploited majority.

5. So far we have deliberately talked in very general terms of popular mobilization and incorporation of the working class into the political process. But such mobilization need not be democratic. In their very different ways, wartime Wilhelmine Germany, Fascism and third world nationalism all testify to that. What makes capitalist democracy at all possible is a characteristic unique among known modes of production. Capitalism is an impersonal mode of exploitation, involving the rule of capital rather than personal domination of the bourgeoisie. It certainly does not function in the manner of an automatic machine, but it does operate as production for ever

greater profit under conditions of impersonal market competition. The rule of capital requires a state – for both internal and external support and protection – but, as long as it upholds the separate realm of capitalist 'civil society', this state does not have to be managed personally by the bourgeoisie. And in the long history of democratization, bourgeois politicians have learnt the many mechanisms at their disposal to keep the state in harmony with the needs of capital.[41]

6. This last-mentioned feature of capitalism may explain why the impersonal rule of a tiny minority is conceivable in democratic forms – why, for example, the rule of capital is compatible with a labour party government, whereas a feudal aristocracy cannot be governed by a peasant party. But a theoretical possibility is one thing, actual historical dynamics quite another. And we have seen that the fight of the working class for universal suffrage and freely elected government was never by itself sufficient to enforce the introduction of bourgeois democracy. This raises the question whether there are other internal tendencies of capitalism, which, under certain conditions, may generate forces of democratization apart from working-class struggle. One such tendency may be immediately identified. Capitalist relations of production tend to create an *internally competing, peacefully disunited ruling class*. In its development, capital is divided into several fractions: mercantile, banking, industrial, agrarian, big and small. Except in a situation of grave crisis or acute threat from an enemy (whether feudal, proletarian or a rival national state) bourgeois class relations contain no unifying element comparable to the dynastic kingship legitimacy and fixed hierarchy of feudalism. Furthermore, the development of capitalism has usually stimulated the expansion of petty commodity production, before tending to destroy it. Thus, the commercialization of agriculture transformed a self-subsistent peasantry into an agrarian petty bourgeoisie with distinct interests of its own.[42]

In the absence of a single centre, some kind of elective, deliberative and representative political machinery became necessary. Therefore, propertied republics or parliamentary monarchies developed at an early stage in the formation of capitalist states – for example, the Italian, German and Swiss city republics, the United Provinces of the Low Countries, Britain, the United States, France and Belgium (the latter after 1830). This was still a democracy for the bourgeoisie only, and fractionalization of capital has only contributed to a democracy including the rest of the population in conjunction with the other tendencies referred to above. Thus, the decisive role in a number of instances of contingent military defeat shows that capitalism does not necessarily develop forces of sufficient strength to extend the basis of democracy to the masses.

## V. Democracy and Dependent Capitalism

This chapter has dealt only with the development of bourgeois democracy in the advanced capitalist countries. In order to arrive at a global picture of the relationship between democracy and the rule of capital, it would be necessary to relate the above outline to analyses both of the history of bourgeois democracy in the underdeveloped capitalist countries and of the anti-democratic forces present in advanced and underdeveloped capitalism. However, assuming that we have correctly identified the essential pro-democratic tendencies of capitalism, we may be able to conclude by tentatively suggesting a few factors that explain the rareness of bourgeois democracy in underdeveloped capitalist countries.

The external inducement of capitalism has had three crucial effects on the bourgeoisie of these countries. First, it has severely restricted the internal differentiation of the capitalist class, making it instead largely dependent on one external centre (factor 6 above). Secondly, the lopsided, externally dependent growth of petty and generalized commodity production has rendered the economic base extremely fragile and vulnerable to international crises, thus leaving the indigenous bourgeoisies little room for manoeuvre vis-à-vis the exploited classes (factor 4). The frequent intertwining of capitalist with feudal, slave or other pre-capitalist modes of exploitation, as well as the combination of enclave capitalism with subsistence farming, has impeded the development of the impersonal rule of capital (factor 5) and a free labour market, thereby seriously limiting the growth both of the labour movement (factor 1) and of a small agrarian and petty bourgeoisie (factor 6).

Furthermore, the national struggles outside Europe, and the European settlements overseas, took place on premises very different from those in Europe. Particularly important in this context was the weakness, in autonomy, culture and organizations of the popular classes, of workers, peasants, artisans, small traders. In the Hispano-American wars of independence they were at most a pool of soldier recruits, for a long time excluded from de facto political rights. By the time of Afro-Asian nationalism, the rhetoric of democracy and techniques of political mass mobilization had developed, but not much the autonomous capacity of the masses of the people. The cultural superficiality of the arbitrarily delineated post-colonial nation-states made them fragile, and the national elites therefore vigilant in containing popular self-organization (factor 1 above).

Those colonies and semi-colonies which have had to wage a people's war to gain their freedom – which entails a class-explicit ideological mobilization – have not fought on a capitalist basis and have subsequently taken a non-capitalist, but also non-democratic road of social development.

## VI. Nation-States, Classes and Democracy

In the last few decades, despite striking *prima facie* evidence to the contrary – European Fascism, third-world military dictatorships, and the like – functionalist and/or evolutionist conceptions of a 'normal' relationship of correspondence between the rule of capital and bourgeois democracy have quite often informed the analyses of both Marxist and non-Marxist writers. My historical examination of the political constellations in which democracy was established in the major and most advanced capitalist countries has revealed the inadequacy of such general arguments and explanatory hypotheses.

Nevertheless, bourgeois democracy is no mere accident of history, and capitalism does contain a number of tendencies which are conducive to processes of democratization. Thus, it has frequently, and correctly, been observed that bourgeois democracy entails a competitive division within a basic framework of unity – even if this statement is interpreted in a naively idealistic way, by reference to ideology and varieties of 'political culture'. But the concrete economic and political dynamic of the rise of capitalism does involve the struggle for and development of a new divided unity. This appears as the *nation-state*, freed of the barriers and boundaries of dynastic legitimacy, feudal enfeoffment and provincial tradition. The establishment of national sovereignty and unity resulted from struggles against royal absolutism, foreign dynasties and provincial separatism.

These were the stakes of the Dutch wars against Spain in the sixteenth and seventeenth centuries; the seventeenth-century English revolution and civil war; the US Declaration of Independence; the French Revolution of 1789; the 1830 August revolution in Belgium; the unification of Switzerland, Italy, Germany, and of the Canadian, Australian and New Zealand colonies; the Meiji Restoration in Japan; the establishment of the constitutional Eider state in Denmark; the emancipation

of Norway and Finland; and even the constitutional struggles within the Habsburg Empire. Only in Sweden, with its
long-standing national unity and peculiar mixture of estates
and Parliament dating from the eighteenth century, were anti-
dynastic and anti-parochial national struggles not a central
component of the nascent process of democratization. But
even in this case, the process exhibited a crucial dimension of
conflict between national and non-national (dynastic, foreign
or provincial) elements: Carolingian absolutism fell under the
blows of the Great Nordic War, and the formation of democracy finally reached maturity under the impact of the foreign
revolutionary aftermath of the First World War. The old
Swedish dynastic nation-state acquired its national-democratic
character essentially from external stimuli, including from
seceding Norwegian nationalism.

Freedom of trade and industry created a network of divisive
competitive relationships which ran through the new ruling
class of the unified and sovereign states. The market replaced
the hierarchical pyramid of medieval and absolutist feudalism.
And it was in this unity-division of national state and market
that the process of democratization originated. This happened
fundamentally in one of two different ways. In certain cases,
democracy was first introduced for upper layers of the bourgeoisie (including commercialized landowners), who alone had
the right to vote and form parliamentary or republican governments. Other sections of the bourgeoisie and petty bourgeoisie
were subsequently included in this structure, according to
widely varying tempos and modalities. In a second way, where
the bourgeois revolution stopped half way, democratization
began as a constitutional compromise between the old landowning ruling class – including its apex, the dynasty – and the
bourgeoisie. This system then developed either into a propertied
democracy, as in Scandinavia, the Netherlands and Belgium, or
into a still largely non-democratic form of government based
on an extended franchise, as in Austria, Germany and Japan.

These are, of course, only the principal routes followed by the process, and specific detours such as the Jacobin regime of 1793 also have to be taken into account. But if these routes accurately express the general pattern, as I believe they do, then we may conclude that bourgeois democracy, in the same way as its Athenian predecessor, first arose as a democracy for male members of the ruling class alone. Only after protracted struggle were these rights extended to the ruled and exploited classes as well. Sometimes the ruling class of these early regimes was extremely narrow – for instance, the few *regimentsfähige Familien* (literally, 'families fit to rule') of the Swiss city republics. Sometimes it was fairly broad, as in the United States. But in every case the propertyless were excluded – in the US and the Canadian, Australian and New Zealand colonies as well as in the parliamentary monarchies of Europe. Nor did things change after the American states gained independence; indeed, property as such had a right to representation, whereby joint owners were given a plural vote to share.[43]

Leaving aside Switzerland, where armed male artisans and peasants won democratic rights in a series of violent struggles in the 1830s, '40s and '50s, neither of the two main processes of this first stage led to the establishment of democracy for all adult men, not to speak of the whole adult population. With this one partial exception, then, competitive capitalism has nowhere led to bourgeois democracy as a result of its own positive tendencies. A Marxist analysis of capitalism, however, must take up centrally the contradictions of the system. And it has been the development of the basic contradiction between capital and labour that has carried democracy beyond the boundaries of the ruling class and its props. Thus, the second stage in the struggle for democracy was largely shaped by the emergence of the working class and the labour movement. We have already seen how the capitalist mode of production gives birth to an exploited class with capacities of organized opposition far superior to those of any previous one. In fact, the labour movement fought almost everywhere not only for higher wages and better working conditions, but also for political democracy – either as an end in itself (the British Chartists or the Australian and New Zealand trade-union movement) or as an integral part of the struggle for socialism (the parties of the Second International).

However, the working-class movement was nowhere capable of achieving democracy by its own unaided resources – and this tells much of the strength of bourgeois rule. From the Chartists in the 1840s to the Belgian Social Democrats just prior to, and the Japanese workers just after, the First World War such attempts always resulted in defeat. Only in conjunction with external allies were the non-propertied masses able to gain democratic rights; and it was above all the propertied minorities who in the end answered the critical questions of timing and form – of when and how democracy was to be introduced. Thus, the process of democratization unfolded within the framework of the capitalist state, congealing in the form of bourgeois democracy rather than opening the road to popular revolution and socialist transformation.

## VII. Exclusions

The historical struggle for democracy has been directed primarily against various forms of exclusion. Dictatorships have tended to appear late in the day and, except in Japan, only after a period of democracy or substantial democratic advances. The development of a purely elective mode of government has sometimes been resisted to the point of revolution (France 1830) and military defeat (France 1871, Austria, Germany, Japan), but in other cases it has taken the form of a very gradual evolution of non-constitutional parliamentary practice (Britain and its dominions, Scandinavia, Belgium, the Netherlands). The monarchy has everywhere in the core of capitalism grown into a powerless symbol. 'Corrupt practices' and state intimidation were also eliminated from the electoral process in a fairly undramatic, though uneven manner. However, the inclusion of various social categories in the 'legal nation' has generally been the object of fierce and protracted constitutional struggle.

The principal criteria of exclusion have been class (more or less crudely defined by property, income, occupation or literacy), sex, ethnicity and opinion. There is an interesting sequential pattern here. Originally, the most contested criterion was class, but sex and race have proved to be much more intractable, and opinion has tended to acquire greater significance. The first constitutional battles were usually fought by male members of the same ethnicity over inclusion of particular socio-economic groups. But since the First World War (and the introduction of male suffrage in Japan in 1925) instances of blatant class discrimination have been relatively infrequent: certain American states continued to employ registration requirements, poll taxes and literacy tests which played a certain role in federal elections until 1970; and the first two industrial states – Belgium and Britain – have retained, respectively, an all but powerless House of Lords and class criteria for eligibility to the Senate.

It has been above all the strength and fighting capacity of the working class that have made it difficult and unduly costly to maintain class-based criteria of exclusion. However, the American experience shows that smaller or more weakly organized groups can be fairly easily excluded from participation in the democratic polity of advanced capitalism. This also seems to be a major factor in the obstinacy of sexist and racist exclusion. In fact, the struggle against sexism and racism has been affected by the same general problems as the fight against overt class discrimination. The ruling class has almost invariably opposed inclusion of ethnic minorities and the female half of the population, and neither has had sufficient weight to enforce its demands without the help of external allies. The use of poor ethnic minorities as cheap labour and strikebreakers has often left these groups without any significant support at all. For instance, the very first point of the Fighting Platform of the 1905 conference of the Australian Labour Party called for 'Maintenance of a White Australia'.[44] In the American South, Blacks were abandoned by the abolitionists and only found militant allies again during the ghetto rebellions in the North and the rise of the student and anti-war movements in the 1960s: it was these forces that finally helped to push federal rulers to move against the much weakened southern plantoc-racy. Racist exclusion can also operate in more refined ways than it has in the US. Thus, it could be argued that, even today, Switzerland should not be regarded as a democracy because the Swiss bourgeoisie has been heavily dependent upon immigrant labour-power since the beginning of the century. And these immigrants have been denied any political rights. More gener-ally, since the 1960s, the massive import of foreign workers into Western Europe with no rights of political representation has signified a *de facto* disenfranchisement of an important minority of the European working class.

## Female enfranchisement

Whereas racist exclusion of poor and degraded ethnic minor-ities has been applied with general vigour, the question of female suffrage has given rise to broad discrepancies: in New Zealand women were enfranchised in 1893, in Switzerland not until 1971; in the American South, White women gained the right to vote fifty years before Black men, but in Finland the two sexes achieved it simultaneously in 1906; in France 150 years, and in Switzerland over 120 years separated the first adoption of universal male suffrage from the effective enfranchisement of women, whereas in other countries the gap was much shorter. The dynamics of female enfranchisement is still a largely unexplored territory, requiring special investigation. Here only a few suggestions can be given. First, we should sound a note of caution about some rather common facile explanations. The male constitutional referenda in Switzerland no doubt delayed the attainment of female suffrage after the majority of politicians had been won over; but by itself that does not settle the question of an obstructionist role of male referenda.[45] In a number of western American states, women were given the vote by male referenda as long ago as the late nineteenth and early twentieth centuries.[46] Reference to ideological factors, such as the Catholic religion or Latin 'machismo' is equally unsatisfactory. Why did Catholic Austria grant women the vote fifty years before predominantly Protestant Switzerland, and thirty years ahead of Catholic Belgium? And how is it that the first breakthroughs in Switzerland were made in the French-speaking cantons of Vaud, Geneva and Neuchâtel, while France came later to female suffrage?

There may perhaps be more substance in the demographic thesis of the 'scarcity value' of women. It is indeed worthy of note that female suffrage was first introduced in recently populated settler territories, where women were greatly outnumbered by men. Women had won the vote by 1900 in Wyoming, Colorado, Utah and Idaho, and by the eve of the

**Table 8.** Timing of Female Enfranchisement

| Before First World War | During or after First World War | In aftermath of Second World War | Later |
|---|---|---|---|
| Australia | Austria | Belgium | Switzerland |
| Finland | Canada | France | |
| New Zealand | Denmark | Italy | |
| Norway | Germany | Japan | |
| | Netherlands | | |
| | Sweden | | |
| | UK | | |
| | US | | |

First World War in another seven states, all west of the Mississippi.[47] The women of New Zealand were enfranchised in 1893. Following the example of the more remote colonies of South Australia (1894) and Western Australia (1899), the Commonwealth Franchise of 1903 adopted female suffrage throughout the Australian territories.[48] In Canada, too, the process started during the First World War in the new prairie provinces of Manitoba, Saskatchewan and Alberta.[49] James Bryce pointed out, in his classical study *The American Commonwealth*, that in the first four American states to give women the vote there were a total of 589,000 men to 482,000 women.[50] In 1891 in the whole of Australia (including the more settled colonies of Victoria and New South Wales) the male to female ratio was 2 to 1 in the age range from fifteen to sixty-four.[51]

Although the explanation by 'scarcity value' fits with the democratic effect of increased wartime demand for female labour-power, the correlation is not itself an explanation;[52] in any case, it is of little use in accounting for later variations. We shall probably find it more fruitful to look into the field of political forces for the relative strength of the enemies and supporters of women's suffrage. As to the enemies, the bourgeoisie of the new colonies was not firmly entrenched and had to accept male suffrage also at a very early date. Two major allies came forward. One was the labour movement, which, as we have noted, soon gained considerable strength in Australia and New Zealand. The militant English suffragette organization – the Women's Social and Political Union – was at first intimately linked to the Independent Labour Party.[53] In Finland, universal suffrage was conceded in 1906 following a massive working-class rebellion. And in Switzerland, the general strike of 1918, which was defeated by the full military might of the state, included the call for women's rights in a list of democratic and social (but not socialist) demands.[54]

This social movement in Switzerland, in which the working class remained isolated, also raises concretely the question

**Table 9.** Percentage of Total Female Population Gainfully Employed c. 1930* (Unpaid family workers excluded)

*Female enfranchisement:*

| Before First World War | During or after First World War | In aftermath of Second World War | Later |
|---|---|---|---|
| Australia 20 | Austria 25 | Belgium 17 | Switzerland 29 |
| Finland 25[1] | Canada 12 | France 23[2] | |
| New Zealand 20 | Denmark 27 | Italy 14 | |
| Norway 22 | Germany 22 | Japan 33 | |
| | Netherlands 19 | | |
| | Sweden 29 | | |
| | UK 27 | | |
| | US 17 | | |

Source: *Yearbook of Labour Statistics* vol. 2 (Geneva 1937) for columns 1 and 2.

*Since the data are drawn from national censuses, we should sound a note of caution regarding their comparability. Thus, they are affected by the inclusion of family helpers (the Japanese figure looks suspiciously high), by the age structure, by the frequency of marriage (in turn largely an effect of the male-female ratio) and by the economic structure – a high level of dairy farming, rice growing and labour-intensive industries would result in higher proportions. The relatively low New World percentages seem partly due to the shortage of women available for domestic chores in the agricultural colonies. Nevertheless, bearing these reservations in mind, the table does prove that there is no significant relationship between gainful employment and enfranchisement of women. If we take account of the different branches of female employment, with their varying degrees of social freedom, then this lack is even more striking. Thus, the figures shown in the table for Norway (enfranchisement 1913) and Switzerland (1971) are 22 and 29 per cent respectively. But when we deduct women employed as domestics, the figures fall to 13 and 23 per cent.

[1] The crude figure is 41 per cent, but the unusually high proportion of female entrepreneurs and employees in agriculture seems to indicate that farmers' wives are included. The corrected figure presupposes that the percentage of women farmers was the same as in Germany – which is probably an underestimation rather than an overestimation.

[2] The French census figure included wives helping in their husband's enterprise. The above calculation assumes the same proportion of women entrepreneurs as in Germany.

of bourgeois and petty-bourgeois allies. For female suffrage was not one of the socio-economic concessions made by the government after the breaking of the strike. By contrast, the small bourgeois and petty-bourgeois Populists proved to be crucial allies in the Western United States,[55] as did their Liberal counterparts in Australia, New Zealand and Norway, and the Prohibitionists of New Zealand and the United States.[56] The extreme weakness of these classes in Japan makes it possible to understand the belated and externally induced character of the process of democratization. But how should we account for sexist intransigence in Belgium, France, Italy and Switzerland?

The then prevalent notion that women were more conservative than male workers hardly ever led right-wing political leaders to overcome their sexist prejudices, in the way that Bismarck swallowed his hostility to the working-class vote.[57] However, in some countries, this evaluation of the likely effect of female suffrage loomed large in the considerations of a sizeable section of the progressive bourgeoisie and petty bourgeoisie. One feature common to Belgium, France, Italy and Switzerland is the long and bitter struggle between, on one hand, bourgeois and petty-bourgeois anti-clerical Radicalism and, on the other, a Catholic Church linked to the landowners and the haut-bourgeois Right. As women were held to be more under the sway of the priests, Liberals and Radicals were reluctant to endorse women's political rights. Only in Belgium, in 1919, did Catholic Conservatives themselves call for female suffrage, which was then blocked by the Liberals with support of the Social Democrats. Until the cataclysms of the Second World War, women's rights seem to have been sacrificed on the altar of anti-clericalism.[58]

## Political bans

The fourth criterion of exclusion – unacceptable opinion – is largely a twentieth-century phenomenon, although the Dutch Batavian revolution did not allow people who did not recognize popular (as opposed to dynastic) sovereignty as eligible to vote. Assessments of the legitimacy of various parties did not initially enter into liberal constitutional conceptions, but they began to develop in late eighteenth-century Britain and early nineteenth-century America, and were absorbed in the Habsburg, Hohenzollern and Japanese Empires.[59] The French Revolution and the Paris Commune produced shock waves of panic and repression among the ruling classes of a number of countries. Nevertheless, in the nineteenth century, political discrimination was by and large subsumed under class-based exclusion. It is striking that in none of the countries studied here were the parties of the Second International actually illegalized. (Bismarck proscribed the SPD in the 1880s, but the party was still allowed to present election candidates. The Social Democrats of Tsarist Russia were illegal most of the time.)

In this century, by contrast, bourgeois states have frequently resorted to explicit political exclusion. The entire labour movement was suppressed in Austria, Germany, Italy and Japan, and at various times the Communist Parties have been banned in Canada, Finland, France, the German Federal Republic and Switzerland. In the United States, the party was virtually driven underground in the fifties (it was not explicitly outlawed, but the effect was rather similar since it had to register as an agency of a foreign state, under pain of imprisonment). In Australia a parliamentary majority attempted to impose a ban on the CP in 1951, but this was defeated, first by a High Court ruling and then by a referendum. In summary, we may say that political prohibition has replaced class-based exclusion as the most efficient means of handling a threat posed by the working class, or a section of it.

## VIII. The Two Paradoxes Explained

We are now in a position to confront the two paradoxes with which we started. For Marxists, it will be remembered, the problem appeared as one of explaining how a tiny social minority has come to rule predominantly in democratic forms; while for bourgeois liberal thought, it seemed an insoluble mystery that classical liberals were convinced of the incompatibility of capitalism and democracy, whereas contemporary bourgeois opinion maintains that *only* capitalism is compatible with democracy.

The solution to the Marxist problem is by now fairly clear. Bourgeois democracy has always and everywhere been established in struggle against (hegemonic fractions of) the bourgeoisie, but through political means and channels provided for by the capitalist state. Moreover, when democracy has been threatened or destroyed, the labour movement has taken up the struggle anew against the leading fraction of the ruling class (as in Austria, Finland, France, Germany and Italy). Thus, although bourgeois democracy is democratic government plus the rule of capital, its democratic component has been achieved and defended against the bourgeoisie.

The bourgeois paradox is resolved when we grasp a feature of the process to which classical liberalism quite naturally paid scant attention. Democracy developed neither out of the positive tendencies of capitalism, nor as a historical accident, but out of the *contradictions* of capitalism. Bourgeois democracy has been viable at all only because of the elasticity and expansive capacity of capitalism, which were grossly underestimated by classical liberals and Marxists alike.

However, democracy has not become the only contemporary political form of capitalism. Democracies are part of a much wider universe of bourgeois states. By reference to the two fundamental dimensions – mode of national representation and inclusion of the adult population in the political process – we have distinguished four major types of bourgeois regime: democracies, liberal exclusivism, authoritarian exclusivism, and dictatorships. We have seen all four in my survey of seventeen core countries of capitalism.

While evolving with the mode of production, the politics of capitalism remains embedded in the variable moulds and different contingencies of nation-states. It is resistant to ideological flatness, even when covered by it, remaining complex and intriguing, thereby attractive to scholarship and to scholarly critique – and necessary to understand for those of us who are fighting the human ravages of capital.

# 3

# The Right to Vote and the Four World Routes to/through Modernity

The present work takes as its starting-point two earlier studies.[1] The aim is to grasp the historical patterns of the emergence, and blockages, of universal suffrage in the modern world. The rise of democracy merits a three-dimensional approach: globally encompassing, in a sense meaningful to actors in the world; historically oriented, with an eye both for concrete processes and for broad, connecting, epochal interpretation; and, thirdly, having a clear focus on political institutions.

The other entrance to this chapter may look something like the following. Modernity has become a common global phenomenon. But the routes to, and the routes of experience through, modernity have differed vastly across various parts of the world. The windows of the well-kept museum of classical sociology, built around conceptualizations of the contrast between pre-modernity and modernity, have to be thrown open to the fresh air of change. Furthermore, under the challenge of postmodernism, modernity has become history, and should be approached as such, both in a dialectical understanding of its inner contradictions, and in empirical investigations of its manifold expressions. What needs to be developed is a comparative historical sociology of modernity.[2]

One very important structural aspect of modernity is the state. A crucial feature of a *modern state* is that its resources of power are reducible neither to its internal military set-up nor to its parameters of population and territory. The power resources of the modern state depend significantly on its capacity to develop the potentials of the populations and of the territory, through education, recruitment, technological advances and imports, infrastructural construction, and so on.

The modern state is not necessarily democratic. A history of democratization, therefore, is by no means synonymous with one of state modernization. Nevertheless, there is an intrinsic relationship between the two processes. The power and the capacity of the modern state depends importantly and positively on popular participation, and democracy or voting is a major political form of political participation.

From another angle, modernity means, among other things, a new, individual-cum-collective identity, both in the direction of individuality and in that of chosen collectivities, of nation, association, and so on. One important expression of this modern individualism/collectivism is the demand for political rights, for citizenship.

Political modernity can be looked at from either vista. In both perspectives, the right to vote is a central institution of political modernity, symbolically honoured also by all major modern dictatorships.

The history of political modernity has taken four major routes in the world, each with a core set of common experiences across major and minor sub-variants. These routes are not just laid out differently in space and in time. The traffic on them is fundamentally interconnected. Indeed, they can be most easily identified in terms of their interrelated differences.

First, there is the *pioneering European* route, along which what is now called modernity, including modern franchise and democracy, first developed, out of, and in struggles against, indigenous traditions. An auto-centred but world-embedded and world-exploiting development has characterized the European road through modernity. Even all of Europe's major disasters have been self-inflicted: the two world wars, Fascism, the Holocaust, Stalinism.

Secondly, there are the *New Worlds* of settler states, the socio-political outcomes of ruthless overseas conquests and mass migrations in the early modern period: the Americas, White Oceania, and certain islands and coastal regions in other areas, such as Singapore. Pre-modernity was here centred overseas in the Old World, and with the coming of modernity the old order was thrown into the ocean. But impulses of epochal change had also come from the Old World, and throughout modernity a very important part of the New Worlds' experiences has been the difficult but intimate relationships with the mother modernity overseas. The legacy of conquering settlement has also created problems of functional, rather than territorial, inter-ethnic relations, that is, centred on the rights and duties of different ethnic groups in a given area, rather than on the autonomy of territories inhabited or to be inhabited by different ethnicities.

Thirdly, we should distinguish the traumatic experiences of the *Colonial Zone*, stretching from northwestern Africa to Papua New Guinea (and some small islands in the Pacific). Modernity came to the Colonial Zone in the form of alien conquest and destruction. Indigenous political institutions were crushed and, by and large, destroyed. The appropriation of modernity by the colonized was therefore a complicated appropriation of institutions and thought of the conquerors including territorial nationalism and popular sovereignty, while, at the same time, using the former against the latter. The misalignment between the boundaries of the modern states inherited/reconquered from the colonizers and those of linguistic, religious, economic and other identities is another central feature of (ex-)colonial political modernity.

Finally, there is a major course to modernity, which we may provisionally designate as that of externally induced *Reactive Modernization*. The designation refers to polities seriously threatened but never fully subjugated by alien imperialism; polities which managed to survive into the modern world by adopting modern state institutions from abroad and grafting

them on to indigenous rule and indigenous society. Modernization, including modern citizenship rights (but not democracy),
in this case came from above, from rulers in power rather
than from popular struggles. Japan of the Meiji Restoration
is the grand case, and Japan has remained the most successful
example of a non-European route through modernity, later
providing a model for others. The Ottoman Empire, with its
Turkish and Arab successors, and China are other major representatives of this fourth road.[3]

My global overview here will trace the rise of modern suffrage along the above-mentioned four routes, and their most
important ramifications. The state and other institutions of
modernity have also travelled along them. But how much
history will impinge upon contemporary institutions will have
to be left open, for the time being.

## I. European Experiences and Achievements

### The arena and the arsenal of tradition

Bearing in mind the long and widely extended pedigree of
institutions, of elections and political participation in Europe,
it may seem unsurprising that modern democracy should have
been pioneered in Europe. However, what also emerges clearly
from the record is the absence of any open track of historical
evolution, and the lateness of democracy in the modern sense.

Ancient traditions were indeed important, but mainly by
laying out an arena and by providing weapons with which
to fight. That arena and that arsenal favoured a development
of socio-political conflicts into struggles about democratic
institutions. But they did not call tournaments for and against
democracy in the modern sense. Even less did they decide the
winner. A new game had to be invented, and new forces had
to emerge with strength and skill enough to win it.

Europe's links to the unique (though restricted) democracies of Classical Athens and Republican Rome were never really cut off. The conceivability and the actual historical existence of democratic government were part of the classical education that the rulers and political thinkers of Europe all received, once the Middle Ages had settled down. Elective rule was an important part of pre-modern European politics. In fact, the two highest potentates of medieval and early modern Europe were both elected, the Pope and the Emperor: political participation and representation were important, institutionalized parts of post-classical Europe. The early Church Councils provided a crucial link between Antiquity and the Middle Ages, and Germanic law contained a set of mutual obligations between ruler and ruled, and practice included elective monarchies.[4]

The political use of concepts of Roman private law, dealing (mainly) with principal–agent relations was remarkable. Roman business law formed the basis of the concept of *representatio*, and of a very important medieval political notion, 'what concerns all, should be treated and approved by all'. In the European Middle Ages it developed into a central constitutional principle, institutionalized in King–Estates, King–Parliament relations and in city governments.[5]

Two examples will be sufficient to underline the importance of Medieval Europe to the political modernity of the world. One is the medieval background and unbroken institutional continuity of the British Parliament, from which derived in the second half of the nineteenth century, the modern ideas of 'parliamentary government'[6] and, in the twentieth century, 'parliamentary democracy'. The other is the reinvoked memory, in 1789, of the French Estates General – the legislative assembly of different estates – which set in motion the process which in a few years led to the enacting of universal male suffrage. However, European political history exhibits no ascending growth curve of popular participation. Between medieval and modern forms of political participation and constitutional principles, there was the age of absolutism, which, true, was not without certain rights of participation nor without legal boundaries upon the ruler.[7] Earlier, in the Macedonian and the Roman Empires, the ancient democracies had melted away.

Secondly, though unique and amazingly advanced for its time, ancient democracy is not the same as modern democracy. The crucial institutions are different: then popular assemblies and offices rotating among the citizens, by lot or by election; now competitive elections for a government that is representative of popular will. In the eyes of each, the other democracy would appear fake and oligarchic. Modern democracy because of its elected elites of professional politicians, ancient democracy due to its restriction of citizenship to a fraction of the adult population, and to its massive abstentions, which were institutionally taken into account.[8]

Thirdly, the medieval principles and institutions of representation and consent referred to various constituent bodies of the polity, to Lords Spiritual and Temporal, counties, cities, guilds, and so on, to the holders of certain specific rights, not to an aggregate of individuals, having political rights just because of their human status. The estates, and similar recognized bodies, did not represent the country or the people, they constituted the people. The opening political battles of the French Revolution concerned this issue of the estates and the nation.

Finally, modern democratization has had to confront the major issue of the rights of social forces, which previously had hardly any significance. This pertains first of all to free wage-workers, who outside some city communes before the Industrial Revolution carried no political clout and were safely dismissed as servants.[9] Later on, women also gained an existence outside the male-headed household and began to demand rights of their own, rights of political participation inconceivable in ancient democracies, and in medieval assemblies.

## The long century of democratization: 1789–1918

The French Revolution established the nation and the citizen as the new basis of the state. Universal male suffrage was instituted for the first time in the rules of August 1792 governing the elections to the Convention and in the Constitution passed by the Convention in June 1793. British Parliamentary Reform in 1832 established a principle of national representativity, rather than of ancient rights.

Yet, the democratization of Europe was a protracted process, with many reversals. Only by 1919, did the majority of Europe have governments directly arising from unrestricted male suffrage. Women were still political outcasts or officially second-rate citizens in a number of major countries. The first continuous (foreign occupation excepted) male democracy, in the sense of a government arising from and holding office dependent on representatives elected by unrestricted suffrage, emerged in France in 1884, only a century after the French Revolution. The oldest (domestically) uninterrupted European democracy is Norway, dating from 1913.

The democratization process took a long time because it was *resisted*. Established opinion had two main fears concerning a wide suffrage, both quite rational. One was the ignorance, the gullibility and the corruptibility of the lower classes. The other was their rationality, their unity and their lack of deference. Together they provided a good set of arguments and motives for most circumstances.

Walter Bagehot expressed both dangers in his famous commentary, *The English Constitution*. In the first edition, published just before the Act of 1867 which extended suffrage, he was mainly concerned with the former of the two dangers. In his 1872 introduction to the second edition, Bagehot expresses similar fears once more, but adds: 'on the other hand, my imagination conjures up a contrary danger. I can conceive that questions being raised which, if continually agitated, would combine the men as a class together'.[10]

From the perspective of democracy and democrats, the problems were the obverse of Bagehot's fears. That is, the gathering of sufficient power and strength so as to be able to overcome entrenched resistance to a wide franchise and to democracy, and the constitution of a capable and autonomous citizenry. A major part of the difficulties of democratization, in Europe and elsewhere, derives from the logical independence and the frequent non-correlation of those two conditions.

The French Revolution set an example from the beginning. Robespierre climbed to political eminence as an advocate of universal male suffrage, and the latter was instituted. However, in the elections of 1792 to the Convention, the world's first universal male election, more than 90 per cent of the electorate did not take part.[11] The 1793 Constitution was never put into effect, due to the war.

The urban petty bourgeoisie, the intellectuals and the students had become strong, connected and sophisticated enough in sudden moments of crisis to topple, at least temporarily, a number of established regimes. In the breaches that were suddenly opened up, wide suffrage and other democratic institutions were established. But the democrats and other radicals were not strong enough to maintain them for very long. Then the forces of reaction or non-democratic conservatism reasserted themselves.

That was the pattern in France, in Spain in the wake of the vicissitudes of its conqueror, and in Portugal as a consequence of the developments in France and Spain, in the Habsburg and the Hohenzollern lands, and in Piedmont in 1848 and after.

When the democratic movement was wide, broad and sustained, resistance was even stronger. The first such movement in history, the British Chartists, was crushed in the 1840s. The second mass movement for suffrage developed in the second industrialized country, Belgium, and was also violently put down.

On the other hand, the long century of 1789–1918 did contain a trend towards more democratic institutions. It even saw the enfranchisement of almost all adult males in several countries. The development of urban and industrial civil society, of independent farmers and industrial workers kept the more or less *ancien régimes* under constant pressure. Royalist and clerical absolutists were on the defensive everywhere. Some astute political entrepreneurs came to understand that the gullibility of the masses was not necessarily an argument against suffrage. It might also be in its favour.

Suffrage was not enforced by a revolt from the servants' quarter, but was let in through the front door by the new proprietor of the house. Louis Bonaparte, later Napoleon III, broke the French revolutionary cycle. The February Revolution had re-established universal (male) suffrage, and in April 1848, in an 83 per cent turnout, France produced the widest effective election in history by then – 6.9 million voted. In December, Louis Bonaparte was elected president with a huge majority. That gave the revolution a non-revolutionary and non-reactionary issue, of which Bonaparte was soon able to avail himself. After some new radical advances, the conservative parliamentary majority reacted by, among other things, restricting suffrage. Then came 'the 18th Brumaire of Louis Bonaparte', the coup d'état of December 1851.

Its historical novelty and significance was that Bonaparte then re-installed universal male suffrage and used it to legitimate his coup. From then on, suffrage proved to be of use as an *instrument of power and rule*, and not only as a popular, egalitarian *source* of power. The second Bonaparte also pioneered almost opposition-less elections.[12] Until the American elections of 1888 (with a population almost 60 per cent larger), nowhere had more people ever voted than in Napoleon III's Second Empire.[13]

Bismarck was the first to learn. He began to push the idea of universal (male) suffrage as an anti-Liberal Prussian stratagem and as part of his drive for a Prussian Germany. Bismarck's Prussian proposal in 1866 of a new constitution of the German League, the move which led to the war with Austria, included a demand for 'direct elections and universal suffrage of the whole nation'.[14] Prussia won its wars with Austria and France, and a German Reich was set up, with universal male suffrage.

Disraeli's reform of 1867 was a similar, but much more cautious and conservative step. By 1914, the British electorate was, along with the Dutch, the second narrowest of Western and Central Europe that is, after the even more narrow Portuguese electorate where the Republic excluded the mass of illiterates.[15]

Other suffrage advances were made in less devious ways than the Bonapartist. In 1890, the Spanish Liberals reintroduced general male suffrage in Spain, followed by equal (non-weighted) suffrage in 1907. Norway, which in 1815 had the broadest electorate in Europe and which virtually had no aristocracy at all, received full male suffrage in 1898, from a progressive liberal Left (Venstre) government, in a move to pre-empt the new Labour Party. The country became a full-fledged democracy just before the First World War; Denmark during it; while Sweden stood during the war constitutionally somewhere between Germany and the rest of Scandinavia.

In the Balkan antipodes of Scandinavia, with their different but also relatively egalitarian or little differentiated social structure, Greece in 1877 changed the broad suffrage of 1864 into general male franchise. The petty notables who formed the Constituent Assembly of independent Bulgaria refused the advice of their Russian helpers and installed universal male suffrage in the 1879 Constitution of Tarnovo. Serbia got in its 1889 constitution a low economic threshold to voting rights. The Russian 1905 Revolution brought internal democracy to Finland, and, more indirectly, full male suffrage to the Austrian part of Austria-Hungary, largely as an imperial means of blunting the edge of the fighting liberal nationalists of various ethnicities but also as a response to wide popular demands.

The Eastern states of landed autocracy or aristocracy made some concessions to elective principles, but not that many. The 1905 Revolution brought forth a three-class electoral system in Russia. Romania had something similar, and Hungary gained a broader system of tax and education thresholds.

However, the old order persisted almost everywhere in Europe.[16] In terms of political institutions, it did so in two broad respects: either as a set of explicit delimitations of any elective popular powers, mainly by an Upper Chamber represent- ing the *ancien régime* and by monarchical prerogatives, both usually backed up by an aristocratic officer corps and higher bureaucracy; or by systems of oligarchic intimidation and manipulation, propped up by, or alternatively mainly deployed through, the state apparatus. On the eve of the First World War, the two patterns constitute a north-south divide of Europe, running roughly from the Pyrenees to the southern Carpath- ians. North of that line, the former model pertained, polished and parliamentarian in Britain, crude and largely absolutist in Russia. Electoral corruption and manipulation were certainly not unknown in Britain[17] and other parts of northern Europe, but they were clearly waning or disappearing by this time.

The most important aspects of the system south of the border was the fracturing of the old order, which made it inca- pable of keeping a clearly staked out power base of its own, and the abject social dependence upon the oligarchy of a major part of the population. The fracturing made stable oligarchic rule impossible, and the weakness of the population at large made a democratic coexistence with oligarchy also impossi- ble. The most stable and peaceful form of political contest and change that these countries developed before the times of Salazar and Franco was a remarkable caricature of British parliamentarianism, a system of *royal electoral rotation*. The monarch had the power to appoint and to dismiss a cabinet.

Let's look at this model: at time *t*, the monarch (or the powers behind him) dismisses cabinet A, and appoints cabinet

B. Cabinet B, which at time *t* only has a minuscule base in Parliament, then calls new elections, whereupon it gains a huge majority with a little help from the state apparatus. At time *t* + 1, the monarch dismisses cabinet B and appoints cabinet A. Prime Minister A then calls an election, and so on. In the late nineteenth century, Portugal, Spain, Bulgaria and Romania developed these features. Romania in the inter-war period made this kind of politics into a fine art.[18] Southern Italy meanwhile had more regionalized forms of managing elections.

Only the World War dealt a fatal blow to the old order in most of Europe. It did so in two ways. The mobilization for industrial war strengthened the position of the working class and the population at large in every belligerent country. Workers' efforts were crucial. Secondly, the military outcome of the war crushed all the strongest and most powerful rulers of the old order, the regimes of the Romanovs, the Hohenzollerns and the Habsburgs. However, in southern Europe the effects were minimal.

## Alternative representations

In the process of revolution overthrowing the old order, a new form of popular representation developed and briefly flourished, the councils of workers, soldiers and peasants.[19] In Russia in 1917 it was a massive movement, in permanent motion at the local level. It seems that in the elections of the delegates to the First All-Russian Congress of Workers' and Soldiers' Councils more than 20 million people participated.[20] Peasants (out of uniform) constituted about a quarter of the electorate, but there was also a separate peasant congress, and the permanent executives of the two established a practice of joint sessions. Together, these soviet movements made up what then was conceived as 'the revolutionary democracy'.[21] The elections to the Constituent Assembly took place with universal suffrage. Only after it became clear that they had lost a majority of their own – though 78 per cent voted for Socialist parties – did the Bolsheviks turn against the Assembly. The Bolshevik 1918 Constitution instituted as state organs the system of soviets it had developed in the course of 1917, adding an explicit exclusion of non-workers from voting rights (valid until 1936), but soon this became only the format of one-party rule.

The workers' councils loomed large also in the German Revolution a year later, clearly drawing much inspiration from Russia. The Social Democratic provisional government, to which power had been handed over by the last imperial chancellor, was later officially set up as the executive of the provisional republican executive of the workers' and soldiers' councils. The *State Gazette* (*Deutsche Reichsanzeiger*) declared on 23 November 1918: 'Political power lies in the hands of the workers' and soldiers' councils of the German socialist republic'.[22] The prime political goals of the Social Democratic leadership, however, remained equal suffrage and parliamentary government. In early February 1919, the Central Workers' Council officially conferred its powers upon the recently elected Constituent Assembly.

The partisan and instrumental use of the Bolsheviks' 'all power to the soviets' slogan and the restabilization of conservative forces outside the USSR meant that the council movement made little lasting impact on the actual history of democracy. But in 1917–18, it was the midwife to the birth of a democratic order in Europe. Its illegitimate child, the one-party state, became another model of political participation later exported to Eastern Europe and imported into China and other parts of the world, most frequently into Africa.

The individualist and rationalist principles underlying universal suffrage had never been very congenial to the traditional religions. Most important was the opposition to the rationale of universal suffrage from Catholic forces. The new political and economic crisis opened new possibilities for a right-wing

Catholic roll-back. New authoritarian 'corporatist' constitutions replaced or explicitly restricted principles of elections and of individual suffrage, in Concordate Fascist Italy, in Portugal, in Austria, in Hungary, in Poland and, after the victory of Franco, in Spain.[23] The heartlands of the Counter-Reformation became from the late 1920s an area of principled official critique and rejection of universal suffrage.

## The difficult happy end

Setbacks followed upon the thrust of 1917–19. On the eve of the Second World War, only the northwestern rim of the continent was governed in more or less democratic ways. Not a single one of the successor states, from Greece to Finland, of the old Ottoman, Romanov, Habsburg and Hohenzollern Empires had a democratic regime, though it is true that the Czechs did not have one as the result of occupation by another of the successor states.

However, a historical advance of the continent as a whole had been made. Democratic institutions were largely kept, one way or the other, by the new, modern dictatorships. Mussolini and Hitler both came to power through the constitutional channels of parliamentary democracy. Hitler also kept the electoral law of the Weimar Republic – while excluding Jews from the body of citizens – and even used it (without, of course, leaving any free choice) in three Diet elections and in two referenda. The Italian Fascists initially (before later corporatism) created a law ensuring that the party with the most votes received a two-thirds parliamentary majority, a system soon imported into Romania and Yugoslavia.

The, so far, happy ending of the European story of the right to vote came in three waves. First, the defeat of Fascism and its reactionary allies in the Second World War redemocratized part of Central Europe and Finland, and gave Belgian, French and Italian women the right to vote. Second, disastrous wars by Greece and Portugal and the death of Franco and of his designated successor opened up a democratization of Greece and the Iberian peninsula in the second half of the 1970s. Swiss women were enfranchised less dramatically (in 1971). Finally, in 1989–91 the Communist one-party regimes crumbled in Eastern Europe after new reform Communists had loosened the Kremlin reins, leading to a flood of demands for choice, and to new political alternatives. The Mediterranean democratization signified the final defeat of the forces of anti-modernity; the Eastern Europe one that the Communist vehicle to socio-economic modernity had reached a dead end.

## II. Settlers' New Worlds

The independence of the New Worlds from the Old Order may legitimately be called part of a 'democratic revolution'.[24] However, in the final development of unrestricted suffrage – free from the restrictions of who can vote and who can be voted for – most of the New Worlds have been late, if they have arrived at all.

This late-coming holds not the least for the United States, granting democratic rights to virtually all males for the first time only in 1870 (the Fifteenth Amendment to the Constitution), only to limit them soon after. Around two centuries after independence, in about 1970, the US finally became 'a normal modern democracy', in the modest sense that every mature adult person who wanted to vote could do so. Canada achieved virtual democracy fifty years earlier than her southern neighbour.

Spain and Portugal had had no early modern parliamentary revolution, and Ibero-America therefore had no colonial assemblies. The institutions of representation in existence and the notions of it emerging in the first stages of the Hispano-American process of independence, the *cabildos abiertos*, of cities were those of Medieval Europe. The idea of elected provincial assemblies in America arrived in 1810, from Spain with a call from its revolutionary Junta Central, in a desperate situation because of the French invasion of Spain. This lack of a colonial electoral politics was certainly a heavy mortgage on the independent states of Latin America and their chances of democracy. But the old order was crushed in the wars of independence (except in Brazil), while it was restored in Europe, although precariously. It was only by the time of the First World War, or soon thereafter, that a series of (male) democratic elections began in Argentina and in Uruguay.

Alone of the New Worlds, Australia and New Zealand have had a political development that might have been expected, that is, rapidly developed, achieved early by world time standards, around the turn of the last century, and stable, without reversals.

Three basic problems made the growth of democracy in the New Worlds much tougher than a Whiggish evolutionism might lead one to believe. First, the difference between democracy in the modern, industrial society sense, on the one hand, and, on the other, in the sense of seventeenth- and eighteenth-century progressive politics had to be overcome. Second, with the colonial order thrown off, a new socio-political order had to be settled, a tremendous task in war-devastated Hispanic America, not to speak of Haiti. Third, inherent in the newness of the New World was an ambiguity to be clarified: Who are we, the people, as distinct from the Others?

## Political side-shows and social indicators

The Constitution of the United States left the suffrage for the states to decide, while granting the Federal Congress a power of altering legislation. No state had, nor did anyone at the time of independence grant, universal male suffrage, not even of unqualifiedly free men.[25]

The complicated, but as a rule, undramatic process of suffrage extension in the United States during the first half of the nineteenth century seems to have been due to three major factors. To begin with, even if not universal, the inherited colonial suffrage was quite extensive for the time, a half or more of white adult males.[26] Secondly, in contrast to the French, the Americans finally won everything, the Revolution, the war and the peace. The old rulers disappeared for good, and the multiple institutions of popular political participation made it very difficult for any new ones to entrench themselves against the rest of the revolutionary coalition. Thirdly, for about three quarters of a century, no new major social forces or issues emerged. Therefore, the working of competitive politics could slowly erode existing privileges, reducing or dispensing with them as by-products of pragmatic problem-solving of other issues.[27]

But the relations of class and suffrage also differed between Old Europe and the New Worlds in another way. No country outside Europe has made the social trajectory from an agrarian, to an industrial, and then to a service society, in the sense of relatively predominant employment. The New Worlds went from an agrarian society to one more or less strongly dominated by so-called tertiary employment.[28] The issue of the franchise and the industrial working class – with its distinctive powers, in comparison with other nonestablished classes, of autonomy, collectivity, skills and disruptive economic potential – was also for this reason never and nowhere posed in the New Worlds – or in the other two regions of global political modernity – as starkly as it was in Europe.

In ways and for reasons different from those of the United States, Latin American development was also gradual, indirect and oblique. Independence started differently south of the border of Anglo-America. In Luso-America the old order was simply nationalized monarchy, dynasty, aristocracy, slavery and all – as the Empire of Brazil. In Hispanic America, fifteen years of devastating wars, both triggered off and finally won by the vicissitudes of the Spanish political theatre, not only destroyed the old order, they also fractured or undermined any new one.

In none of the first wave of Latin American constitutions was there universal male suffrage.[29] Characteristic of all the early and most of the nineteenth-century Latin American constitutions, including the Brazilian one of 1824, was a system of indirect elections, starting at the level of the parish. It derived from the Cádiz Constitution of the Spanish Empire in 1812, in the making of which American delegates also participated. This introduced an oligarchic, demobilizing moment into the core of the electoral system. It also made the suffrage extension less explosive.

Elite cosmopolitan sophistication and mass quiescence made possible undramatic advances of suffrage rights in the interstices of *caudillo* dictatorships and civil wars. In the 1850s at least three Latin American countries adopted constitutional provisions for universal male suffrage: Colombia in 1853 – leading to one brief spurt of participation in a presidential election, in 1857; Venezuela in 1857, which in fact only came to be used in the elections to a new Constituent Assembly in 1858; and Mexico in 1857, where it was used in a series of more or less regular indirect elections. Only in Mexico did suffrage arise from a political upheaval, a liberal revolution of 1855, *La Reforma*.[30]

The dramatic moments of electoral law change in Latin America have not been establishments of universal rights, but of the free exercise of existing rights. 'Effective suffrage and no re-election' was the slogan that launched the most profound and protracted social struggles of the New Worlds since the Wars of Independence, the Mexican Revolution of 1910. Fair elections, with male suffrage, were also the achievements of the Argentine Sáenz Peña Law of 1912 and of the Uruguayan constitution of 1917, both landmarks of each country's political history.

The low uptake of suffrage rights has meant that the non-democratic exclusivism of rulers is more obvious in Latin America than in Europe. It wasn't until 1988 that the principle of universal suffrage became constitutionalized in all of Latin America, with its introduction in Brazil (dispensing with the significant illiterate exclusion). All adult Chileans got the right to vote only in 1970, Ecuadorians and Peruvians in the course of the 1970s.

Between the mid-nineteenth century and the 1970s or 1980s, electoral participation in the Americas was low in comparison with Europe, with the exception of Peronist and post-Peronist Argentina, which picked up in the early 1950s.[31]

### Boundaries of the people

Are natives of a conquered land part of the people or not? And If so, are they a major or minor part?[32] By definition all New World countries are countries of immigration. Where should the line be drawn between the immigrant citizen and the alien immigrant? Hispanic America on the eve of the Wars of Independence had a population of which about 45 per cent were Indians, around 30 per cent Mestizos, 20 per cent White and 5 per cent Black.[33] In spite of this ultimately politically open-ended mix, and despite a number of ethnic rebellions and racist reactions just before and occasionally in the early phases of the Wars of Independence, ethnic boundaries have had a remarkably minor influence upon democracy in Latin America. Instead of becoming sharp foci of racist boundaries between the people and the Others, as in North America, Australia and South Africa, race and ethnicity in Latin, and in particular continental Hispanic, America became more a part of the class structure of the people. Ibero-American society was permeated by hierarchy, that is, by gradation and experience in coping with it. Bolívar had, when in desperate need, turned to the Black republic of Haiti for help, and got it, in exchange only for a promise to abolish slavery, which he tried to keep.[34] But he was more than an abolitionist: 'Let us remember that our people are ... a compound of African and American elements', he said in his most famous political oration, at a time of triumph.[35] Constitutionally, literacy and property qualifications, and the intricate system of indirect elections, were sufficient to keep the masses at bay by legal means, and, if need be, the *haciendados* and the *caudillos* had other means as well.

The leaders of North American independence had made no concessions on slavery, and with the extension of White suffrage, the exclusion of free Blacks spread. By 1858, 'the suffrage was denied to free Negroes in an overwhelming majority of the northern states'.[36] The Civil War against the slave states did alter northern conceptions of Black rights but in the South the new colour-blind suffrage was no more than a brief military diktat. After 1896, Blacks were almost completely disenfranchised, and at the same time the political participation of poor Whites was also severely restricted.[37] The suffrage restrictions in the Southern United States were in their severity second only to those of the Bourbon Restoration in France in 1815. After the Second World War, Black voter registration started to grow in the southern states of the US. The increasing weight of Blacks in the North gradually provoked some Federal concern at the absence of democracy in the South. In the 1960s, the right to vote became a central political issue in the United States, a right finally won after a protracted struggle against violent resistance.

The political rights of new immigrants were the target of restrictive measure in the northern states of the US after 1896, with the (re-)introduction of literacy tests and with tightened individual pre-voting registration. In this way, a large number of new immigrants never got to vote, and US political participation rates fell off.[38] The effects of this demobilization remain, mainly sustained today by the registration system. The immigrant issue was most important in Argentina, which had the proportionately largest influx into the Americas. By the time of the introduction of universal male suffrage in Argentina, 53 per cent of all adult males in the country were non-citizens.[39]

## III. The Colonial Zone and its Emancipation

The Colonial Zone successfully maintained its indigenous ethnicity, but political continuity was completely lost. In most cases territorial continuity was lost as well. In sub-Saharan Africa, only Botswana, Burundi, Rwanda and Swaziland have a continuous territorial history, whereas a pattern of precolonial territorial identity clearly prevails on the Southeast Asian peninsula, from Myanmar to Vietnam. Colonial rule consolidated only after the independence of (most of) the New Worlds. Freedom from foreign rule was obtained in this huge area in a rather compressed period of about two decades, from the late 1940s to the mid-1960s. In contrast to the American Wars of Independence, constitutional handovers made up the predominant, if not the only, form of access to national independence.

Democracy in the context of decolonization was a three-cornered issue: one corner pertained to the relations between the colonized and the colonizer; another concerned the class or stratification relations of the colonized; and a third centred on the latter's ethnic and religious relations. The first was inherent in the situation of invasion and conquest, but it was given a particular dimension because of the colonial relation. Intrinsic to the third, as far it became institutionalized, was a recognition – however silent or qualified – of the superiority, in some respects, of the colonizer. Thereby the attractiveness of many of his institutions and of his language, and of immanent critiques of the actual deployment of colonial arrangements. The class or stratification relations of the colonized acquired a particular dynamic from the new sources of wealth, power and prestige created by the colonial society. Thus, not only were existing systems of stratification undermined, new rival ones were also emerging. Thirdly, to old conflicts between ethnicities and religious communities were added and superimposed new ones from the colonial disruption of pre-colonial territories, economies, polities and cultures.

From the perspective of institutional history, modern politics in the Colonial Zone developed in four common stages, of widely varying forms and interrelations. First, there was the colonial subjection, erosion, transformation and reuse of the old authorities. The latter were hardly ever completely destroyed, but were recognized de jure with certain powers and ceremonial rights. Second, a new political framework was set up by the colonial government, thereby defining the territory, language, constitution and administrative and judicial apparatus of a new politics. In this context, it is noteworthy that this framework, sometimes from very early on, as a rule came to include a central representative body of some sort, attached to the local centre of the colonial power. Thirdly, institutions and practices of mass politics developed: collective action, organized parties, and in most cases wide-franchise elections, representative government. In some colonies, however, the eruption of mass politics was met by unyielding repression, leading to anti-colonial war, such as in French Vietnam, Dutch Indonesia and Portuguese Africa. Finally, there is the achievement of national independence and the establishment of modern national political institutions.

### The rise of representation[40]

The constructive beginning of modern politics in the colonies was usually the establishment of a colonial council, in the British colonies called a legislative council. Normally they started out as advisory to the Governor and more or less completely appointed by the colonial power. The colonial councils were generally meant as a resource for the Governor, and also as a way for the metropolitan Colonial Office to check on him. These small and weak bodies were of great historical importance, because they became the focal point of the new political nationhood. The early attempts at armed rebellion were all crushed and repressed. Therefore, to radicals and moderates alike, the composition, the powers and the decisions of the colonial council became a rallying-point for nationalist politics.

In the British Empire, the colonial Legislative Council has a long history. In India, the 1833 Charter Act established an All-India Legislature in 1853 separated from the colonial executive. Three Indians were appointed to it in 1863, and in 1892, at the demand of the Indian National Congress, indirectly elected members were added. Ceylon (now known as Sri Lanka) also gained its Legislative Council, in 1833, into which the Sinhalese, the Tamils and the Dutch-Eurasian 'Burghers' had one appointed representative each, and the European planters and merchants three. Only in 1910 was the elective principle introduced into the legislature of Ceylon, with a narrow franchise of literacy in English qualifications. When the Straits Settlements of Malaya ceased to be colonially governed from India in 1866, a Legislative Council was set up there, too.

In 1887, the French set up a Conseil Supérieur de l'Indo-chine with limited advisory functions and minority Vietnamese representation. Vietnamese deputies were elected to the lower councils of Cochin-China, Annam and Tonkin, under an extremely narrow franchise somewhat widened in 1922. The Dutch had brought the Indonesian archipelago under unified colonial rule by 1898. In 1918 an advisory People's Council was instituted, originally with minority Indonesian representation. Some years later it acquired some legislative competence and a slight non-European majority.

In West Africa, too, the colonial councils started early, in Nigeria in 1862, on the Gold Coast in 1874. The first African was appointed to the latter in 1888, in Nigeria in 1901. In the early 1920s, restricted elections to a minority of the seats on the Legislative Council were introduced in British West Africa, with the first Africans elected in Nigeria in 1923, in Sierra Leone in 1924, and on the Gold Coast, in today's Ghana, in 1925.

The French Revolution had, in 1793, given citizenship to all inhabitants of France's colonies. When France started to accumulate colonies again in the nineteenth century, this principle was not followed. However, in the four urban communes of present-day Senegal, African citizenship survived, although in restricted form. As in Europe and in Canada, the needs of war mobilization led to a final recognition of citizenship rights in the 'four communes' of Senegal. In 1920, a General Council for all Senegal was established, half of it elected by the citizens and half by the chiefs. In the course of the 1920s, elected minorities, under very restrictive franchise, were added to the councils of the other French colonies of West Africa. French West Africa and French Equatorial Africa were ruled as two large blocs, but only in 1947 were elected colonial councils set up on that level.

In British East and Central Africa, constitutional developments came later, apart from settler elections in Kenya and Zambia in the 1920s. Direct elections of African representatives on the Legislative Council there took place only from 1957, appointed African councillors had appeared since 1945. The Belgian Congo had no elections before the municipal elections to the largest cities in 1957, conducted under an official (but not very effective) ban of parties and lists.[41] The Belgian UN trusteeship over Rwanda-Burundi was carried out by indirect traditional rule, and a system of partial and indirect elections to a Superior Council of the Country was only installed in 1953.[42]

Once councils had acquired an indigenous, more or less elected character, they had a relationship to the colonial power which in some respects resembled that of nineteenth-century

European Parliaments to the monarchic regimes of that time. But there were several crucial differences. The stakes of metropolitan power and privilege were less than at home, and with internal democratization of the metropoles the range of colonially ruling opinions widened. The accumulated experiences of vast empires, such as the British and the French, provided an intellectual and administrative capital which the constitutional monarchies could not muster against domestic opposition. The colonial opposition, on the other hand, faced the incomparably more difficult tasks of learning to master a foreign political culture, bringing it to the people against the powers of local traditional authorities and using it to oust the incumbents – the colonizers – who had brought it in the first place.

No wonder, then, that the two strong imperial powers for a long while kept most of the initiative in the constitutional development of the colonial polities, meaning that mass politics was slow to develop.

The Indian National Congress was a pioneer and a pace-setter for modern nationalist politics in the world's largest colonial empire. It began as a very moderate manifestation of Westernized elite politics. Electoral rights could be granted only to people with the proper education and income.[43] Congress does not seem to have played any significant part in the Government of India Act of 1919, which provided a large, if still restricted, suffrage.[44] It turned to mass politics after the First World War. The (Motilal) Nehru Report of 1928 and its adopted proposals made universal suffrage official Congress policy.

An all-British commission drafted a new Indian constitution which was passed by the British Parliament and critically received by almost all Indian parties. Its introduction of responsible provincial governments, with a franchise broadened to 30 million did materialize, while communal deadlock made the complicated provisions for central government unworkable. Qualifications differed among the provinces, using literacy, tax payment, service in the armed forces and other criteria. Literate women or women married to enfranchised males could vote. Apart from the general constituencies, there were special ones for the ethnic-religious communities, for women, for low castes, and for corporatist 'representatives of commerce and industry, landholders, and ... labour'.[45]

## Disjunctures of suffrage and independence

Sri Lanka, then known as Ceylon, was the first colonial country to gain universal suffrage, in 1931, earlier than many European and American countries. The proposal was made by a British commission, improved by the London Colonial Office. The Ceylon National Congress deputation to the commission made it clear that they wanted a restricted franchise, with an income threshold, and that women might be allowed the vote only if qualified by literacy or property. True, there was a not insignificant Ceylonese movement, which in the 1920s had been calling for male suffrage, also organizing the Ceylon Labour Union. But progressive British opinion on the commission was decisive.[46]

In the rest of colonial Asia the impact of the First World War was much less. No enduring mass politics developed. Localized rebellions in the Dutch East Indies, in French Vietnam and in Burma were easily crushed and followed by widespread repression and vigilance. Vietnamese hopes of change with the French Popular Front petered out in bitter disillusionment with the puncturing of the progressive balloons in France itself.

It was the Japanese attack and occupation which changed the whole situation of the region and encouraged nationalism everywhere, both anti- and pro-Japanese.[47] The Dutch and the French tried to recover their lost colonies, and lost again in colonial wars. The British pulled out of Burma, but they finally defeated an ethnically isolated although strong Communist guerilla movement in Malaya and could hand over to an ethnically well-managed conservative coalition.

In Sub-Saharan Africa, mass politics arrived only after the Second World War. In the Gold Coast and Nigeria, the British government introduced new constitutions, for the first time creating a majority of African non-officials on the Legislative Council. But this was now too little. The southern nationalists in Nigeria staged a massive campaign against the new constitution, not least against the role allocated to the chiefs. On the Gold Coast, mass riots suddenly altered the political landscape. After elections in 1951, Ghana gained colonial Africa's first elected cabinet government. Prime Minister Nkrumah put through a wide, direct suffrage in 1954, extended to universal suffrage in 1956. Continuous nationalist pressure moved Nigeria's constitutions ahead. In the last pre-independence elections, in 1959, there was universal suffrage in the East and in the West, and male suffrage in the Muslim North.

In French West Africa, mass politics also developed in the 1940s, but very much to the rhythm of metropolitan French politics, in which the African leaders took an active part. The suffrage was considerably broadened in 1946, and even more so in the ensuing years. Finally, in 1956, came universal and equal suffrage in all French Africa. The immediate background was not extra Black mobilization, but the war in Algeria. The suffrage was an anticipatory move, although it had both been demanded and bureaucratically planned before the election of the new left-wing government in Paris. Black Africa got what it wanted then, even, after some wrangling, parliamentarily responsible governments in the territories, now overtaking the eminence of the vast colonial divisions, Western and Equatorial Africa.

Electoral participation was relatively high in post-war French Africa. In 1957 between a fifth and a third of the population voted in France's sub-Saharan colonies. Mobilization was lower in Ghana, with 11–12 per cent in 1954 and 1956, and in Nigeria in 1959 the vote was 16 per cent.[48]

In East and Central British Africa, the suffrage was finally precipitated by developments in the rest of the continent and established in the first half of the 1960s.[49] In Tanganyika, for instance, a new constitution in 1960 launched an election with literacy and income qualifications, as well as special and strongly overrepresented seats for Europeans and Asians. The landslide victory of TANU (the Tanganyika African National Union) then led to independence and to universal suffrage.

Democracy and universal suffrage were hardly the major means to achieve independence, where this was gained without war. Indeed, in most of the cases where national independence was put to a direct electoral test, it lost. Where universal suffrage post-dated independence, it was not the major issue in the final decolonization process. However, it could well be argued that the suffrage was more important in the decolonization process and to its major protagonists than it was to the creation process and to the leaders of the Eastern European successor states to the dynastic empires, and of the New Americas.

Electoral mass politics was the medium through which the major leaders and the major political parties asserted themselves and rose to power. It was on the basis of their successes in electoral mass politics that Nehru, Jinnah, Abdul Rahman, Nkrumah, Azikiwe, Touré, Houphouët-Boigny, Nyerere and others could finally make their successful demands for national independence. It was in broad, competitive elections that later ruling single parties first established themselves.

The Indian elections of 1946 took place under a restrictive franchise. They were crucial in reconfirming Congress as the dominant political force and in expressing the new hold of the Muslim League of the Muslim constituencies. Communal relations and Pakistan secession were the central issues of conflict in the final phase of decolonization.

The 1949 constitution of independent India provided for universal suffrage. India and what was then Ceylon (now Sri Lanka) have maintained it, although in an occasionally strained manner, ever since. Burma, now Myanmar, had suffrage in progress until the military coup of 1962. In Pakistan, no new constitution could be completed and put into effect, and therefore no national elections (only regional ones) could be held, before the army, after its defeat in Bangladesh, lost the power it took in 1958. The Federation of Malaya received its first elected Legislative Council in 1955, held an election which constituted its governing ethnic-political alliance, and gained its independence with universal suffrage in 1957. The first general elections were held in 1970. Indonesia had its first elections in 1955, until 1999 the only ones under basically unrestricted suffrage. The Geneva Agreements which ended the first colonial war in Vietnam, stipulated elections, but they never took place. Instead, a second war ensued.

The model of British Africa may be said to have been set in the Gold Coast in the early 1950s. Zimbabwe and later Namibia represented a special variant, because of settler power and guerilla warfare. International pressure finally pushed through a negotiated transfer of power, with a plural set of African negotiators. Negotiated and supervised elections then decided to whom, and to some extent under what conditions, the transfer should take place.

French Black Africa developed a remarkable pattern of its own. Under the 1956 rules of universal suffrage, national independence was put to a referendum in September 1958. Independence was voted down, in eleven of twelve territories.[50] Less than a year after the referendum, however, Senegal's leader, Léopold Senghor, declared he was in favour of negotiating independence, and in June 1960 Houphouët-Boigny of the Ivory Coast did the same. Even with disciplined party organizations, elevated political leaders have to adapt to the times of nationalism if they want to stay in the game.[51] Independent Ivory Coast and Senegal have also been among the most stable African states if not the most pluralist, with some of the highest electoral participation rates.[52]

## IV. Reactive Modernization

*Popular elections as means to national power*

The basic pattern of suffrage development and democratization in the non-European polities surviving the height of European and US imperialism was formed by the adoption of elective institutions as a means to preserve their independence and to enhance their international position. The sparks were the demands and the threats of dangerously successful powers, endowed with central elective representative institutions.

Political thought of the non-European major civilizations was not devoid of concepts and reflections of rule by deliberation and consent and of decision by election. The last of the Seventeen Articles Constitution, attributed to Japanese Crown Prince Shotoku (early seventh century AD, and historically documented at least by 720) says: 'Matters should not be decided by one person alone. They should be discussed with many others ... It is only in considering weighty matters ... that many others should be involved in debate and discussion so as to arrive at a reasonable judgment.'[53] The Charter Oath, the main constitutional document of the Meiji Restoration in 1868, was formulated in a circle of nobles who knew of US and British representative institutions, but government through deliberation was not alien to Japanese feudalism, to whose lords the first drafts of the proclamation directly referred. The first article of the Oath issued by the emperor ran: 'Deliberative assemblies shall be established on an extensive scale and measures shall be determined by public discussion.'[54]

Classical Sunni Islam developed a political theory in which consultation, *shura,* was considered central to Islamic principles of government, and which also debated proper forms of electors and elections, of the Khalifa, the Prophet's successor, the highest authority in the state, and of the relations between the ruler and the community of Muslims.[55] This was a legacy which nineteenth- and twentieth-century Muslim thinkers and jurists could, and did, go back to. As Bernard Lewis has underlined, the birth of Islam provides the language and imagery for modern Islamic political thought in a way similar to the role of the Roman Republic for the Jacobins and the French Revolution for the Bolsheviks.[56]

But the problem was that even these traditions provided no existing institutions, not even a concrete models of any.[57] Only the least statified of the surviving non-European polities, the Afghan – independent from Persia only since the mid-eighteenth century – had something which might be called a representative institution, the irregularly summoned Loya Jirga, a large consultative assembly of ethnic, clan and religious leaders.[58]

The Ottomans, the first to be threatened, by European imperialism, were also the first to inaugurate representative reforms. Indeed, in the history of democracy, the Ottoman Empire preceded its Russian enemy. A decree calling for the establishment of administrative councils with an elected majority in every major administrative sub-division of the empire was issued in 1840, and came to function, albeit irregularly and with variable results.[59] The initiative came from above, by a high imperial official with diplomatic experience in London and Paris, Reshid Pasha, and the motive was to strengthen the empire by connecting its subjects more closely to the regime.

A palace coup of reform-minded civilian and military officials deposed Sultan Abdulaziz in 1876. The Young Ottomans then drove through a constitution, with an elective imperial assembly. A transitional provision summoned an assembly indirectly elected by the administrative councils. The new Sultan suspended it in 1878, but before that it had passed a new electoral law which was put to use after the Young Turk revolution of 1908. The Ottoman 1877 electoral law was in fact carried over into the Republic of Turkey after the First World War. It provided for indirect elections and originally required voters to be males who paid property tax. The Republic then gradually extended the franchise, to all males in 1923, to women in 1934, and oppositional voters in 1946, when direct elections were also instituted.[60] Participation in the indirect elections was minuscule, between 1 and 2 per thousand of the population in the last decade of the Ottoman Empire.[61]

The Japanese leaders of the Meiji Restoration moved more slowly, but much more solidly than the Young Ottomans. While sometimes falling out among themselves, leading to local samurai uprisings in the 1870s, the Meiji Restoration faced no centre of reactionary power, like that faced by the Palace of Istanbul.[62] The feudal deliberative assemblies that first followed from the Charter Oath fitted very badly with the purposes of imperial modernization, which united all the leaders of the 'Restoration', and were soon allowed to lapse.

In the mid-1870s public debate and organization-building for an elected Parliament started and was further developed. The initiative was taken by the belligerent faction which had urged, in vain, for an invasion of Korea in the early 1870s. Among the forces that counted, there was little or no explicit opposition to the idea as such. All faction leaders agreed 'that it was necessary to have the people satisfied and able to co-operate actively with the administration, in order to reach the goal of modernization and full national sovereignty [for instance, the abrogation of unequal treaties]'.[63] They differed in their views on the tempo of reform, and the model to be imported. The most progressive wing looked to England, those who won, to Germany (although the British constituency system was imported).[64]

An Imperial Rescript of 1881 promised a constitution by 1889 and an elected Parliament by 1890. Both pieces of long-term political planning were fulfilled in due time. The franchise was very restricted, with no women allowed and a relatively high tax payment threshold. Only 4 per cent of adult males were allowed to vote, and 95 per cent of those did.[65] The Japanese electoral turnout in 1890 was proportionally twice as large as that of the last July Monarchy elections in France, and at the same level almost exactly as the Swedish turnout in 1875.[66] A party system, representing the regime spectrum from modernizing conservatism to conservative liberalism, emerged, and between those options, Japan's first election was basically fair, according to historian Richard Mason, and more or less continued to be so. But parties and elections did not constitute the centre of political power before the end of the Second World War.

Wartime inflation and industrialization laid the basis for the surge of a working-class movement after the First World War and for a broad, radical male suffrage movement. It seems that the political class was not hostile to a widening of suffrage,[67] but they did not want to be pushed by the people. Then in 1925, amid general quiescence, male suffrage was passed, together with a Peace Preservation Law, against dangerous radical ideas.[68] Japanese women were enfranchised only after Hiroshima, with the MacArthur Constitution.

Before the Japanese attack in 1895, the Chinese political 'vocabulary of change' does not seem to have included elective representation. But then both reformist democracy and revolutionary conspiracy emerged.[69] After some time, in 1906, an official commission chaired by Prince Chun came to this conclusion: 'The wealth and strength of other countries are due to the practice of constitutional government, in which public questions are determined by consultation with the people. The ruler and his people are as one body animated by one spirit.'[70]

Among literate opinion, constitutional agitation was kept up, and in 1908 the Imperial Court announced a Chinese Nine-Year Plan of parliamentarization. In 1910, a National Assembly was to meet, half-appointed and half-elected in 1909. After various local government reforms, a National Parliament was to be elected in 1917. The first part of the plan was put into effect.

The franchise was limited. Certain alternative educational qualifications were needed, or a substantial amount of property, and it was restricted to males. Elections were indirect. The electorate came to comprise 1.7 million, 0.4 per cent of the population. The turnout seems to have been well over half, the same as it was in Restoration France of the 1820s.[71] The National Assembly and the surrounding literati agitation forced the Court to bring forward the calling of a Parliament, but in the autumn of 1911, the Revolution broke out.

The Republic lowered the education and property qualifications, and for a brief time, Guangdong province even allowed women to vote and to be elected. For the 1912, still indirect, elections, the electoral rolls included 40 million people, 10 per cent of the population, or 20 to 25 per cent of all adult males. How many voted in the irregular election is not known, and the First Liberal Republic was soon disbanded. The Second also had an election, in 1918, before it came to its ignominious end of blatant parliamentary corruption, in 1923.

From 1909 to 1912 there was an impressive administrative capacity deployed in establishing the electoral registers, and the first election brought forward an important new breed of political actors, crucial in the series of provincial declarations of independence by which the Revolution spread. But the elections could create no new socio-political order, while the old order and its contenders for succession crumbled, or died. The smaller polities of Reactive Modernization will have to be excluded here. [72]

## Coda 2020

The text above first appeared in *State Theory and State History*, edited by Rolf Torstendahl and published in 1992 in London by SAGE Publications. It was the outcome of an international project, initiated by Torstendahl, a Swedish historian, to bring political historians and social scientists together on the topic of the state. It gave me the occasion to take up again, in a global perspective, the studies of the historical development of democracy I had begun in the 1970s, which focused on the core of rich capitalist countries and somewhat later Latin America. The intentions of my contribution were big and ambitious: a succinct global history of elective politics. Understandable editorial space limits cut it down in size, if not in scope.

When wrestling with how to grasp and conceptualize an empirical global history of elective politics, I made a discovery which has guided much of my historical work ever since, elaborated in *The World* (2011) and deployed in *Cities of Power* (2017).

Beneath the myriad paths to a modern nation-state and to modern societies, there is a limited and scholarly manageable set of four major historical routes to modernity, which have had enduring effects to this day. There is the world-embedded and world-exploiting, but self-centered, European trajectory, with its enduing effects of class salience and secularisation, inter alia; the seceding settler states and societies with their centrality of race in conquered and enslaved lands; the ex-colonial emancipation with its lingering postcolonial dualities and its inherited arbitrary cultural heterogeneities; and finally the Reactive Modernization of threatened but non-conquered countries and their attempts to preserve the traditional realm by instrumental modernization. Each of the first three routes has two major lanes: Western as distinct from Eastern Europe; the British (and other north-western European) settlements and their Iberian counterparts; ex-colonial Africa and ex-colonial Asia. The countries of Reactive Modernization, on the other hand, are most easily distinguished by success (Japan) and variations of non-success (the others).

I have later come to think of the four routes to modernity, both as empirical pathways and as ideal types. That is, a given country might develop into modernity by taking two or more of the main historical roads, or perhaps more adequately, by taking their vehicles. This hybridity characterizes the two big powers outside of the North Atlantic orbit, Russia and China. Russia was an integral part of Europe, its monarchy, its aristocracy, its capitalism and its labour movement. But as a whole it was poor, underdeveloped and threatened by a more developed Western Europe. Reactive Modernization was a crucial lodestar of Russian politics, from Peter I to Lenin and Stalin. Reactive Modernization has also been an aspiration from the late Qing Empire, the early Republic, to Maoism, Deng Xiaoping and his successors. But late nineteenth- and early twentieth-century China was a semi-colony, preyed upon by a pack of imperialist powers. And Chinese modern history cannot be understood without taking into account a third, European element: class politics. It was relayed to China by the Soviet Union and the Comintern, laying the foundations of a political force, very much mutated, but still governing China.

The main message of the text above is not directly civic and political, unlike the others. It has two main messages. One is the joy of scholarship, of exploring the world beyond the one you are born into, beyond the EU and the 'West'. The second message, this one cultural as well as scholarly, is the polycentric making of the modern world. I do not think the idea, elaborated by the great Israeli sociologist Shmuel Eisenstadt, of 'multiple modernities' adds very much to our understanding of the world, although it does form a major advance from the prevailing occidentalist myopia.[73] We all know that contemporary societies differ. Mapping the global pattern of historical development sheds new cognitive light without predetermining our futures.

# Notes

## Preface

1  I made an input to it in a previous work, *The Killing Fields of Inequality*, Cambridge 2013.
2  'The Rule of Capital and the Rise of Democracy', *New Left Review* I/103, May–June 1977.
3  *Science, Class and Society* (1976), *What Does the Ruling Class Do When It Rules?* (1978), *The Ideology of Power and the Power of Ideology* (1980).
4  'The Travail of Latin American Democracy', *New Left Review* I/113, January–April 1979.
5  Adam Przeworski, et al., *Democracy and Development*, Cambridge 2000, p. 49.

## 1. Dysfunctional Democracies

1  See the International Social Survey Programme section of the GESIS website, www.gesis.org.
2  Government economic policy was the most frequently cited cause of inequality, blamed by 29 per cent on average, followed by wages (23 per cent): R. Wike, 'With 41% of global wealth in the hands of less than 1%, elites and citizens agree inequality is a top priority', Pew Research Center, 8 November 2014.
3  World Economic Forum, 'Top 10 Trends for the World in 2015', 7 November 2014.
4  At country level, the figure ranged from over 80 per cent in Mexico (this was before the election of the left wing Andrés Manuel López Obrador to the presidency) as well as in Greece, Brazil and Spain. High dissatisfaction was also found in Italy (70 per cent), South Africa (64 per cent), Argentina (63 per cent), Nigeria (60 per cent), the US (58 per cent) and Japan (54 per cent). Least dissatisfied

were Swedes (30 per cent), Filipinos (31 per cent), Indonesians and Indians (both 33 per cent. R. Wike et al. 'Many across the globe are dissatisfied with how democracy is working', Pew Research Center, April 29 2019.

5  R. Wike, L. Silver and A. Castillo, 'Many across the globe are dissatisfied with how democracy is working', Pew Research Centre, 29 April 2019.

6  Aristotle, *The Politics*, Harmondsworth 1962, p. 155.

7  M. Robespierre, *Déclaration des droits de l'homme et du citoyen*, 21 April 1793, *Discours et rapports à la convention*, Paris 1985. Cf. J. Dunn, *Setting the People Free: The Story of Democracy*, London 2005, chapters 2 and 3.

8  A. Soboul, *Les Sans-culottes parisiens en l'an II*, Paris 1968, chapter 2.

9  I. Murat, *La IIe République*, Paris 1987, p. 99.

10  M. Gribaudi and M. Riot-Sarcey, *1848 la révolution oubliée*, Paris 2009, p. 19.

11  I. Murat, op cit., p. 223.

12  I. Murat op. cit., chapter VI; P. Vigier, *La Seconde République*, Paris 1967, pp. 30ff.

13  J. Lepore, *These Truths*, New York 2018, p. 191.

14  G. Wills (ed.), *The Federalist Papers by Alexander Hamilton, James Madison, and John Jay*, New York 1982, 'The Federalist' no. 10, pp. 45–6.

15  R. G. Parkinson, *The Common Cause*, Chapel Hill 2016, p.169.

16  E. Foner, 'Tremendous in his Wrath', *London Review of Books*, 19 December 2019, p. 13.

17  R. G. Parkinson, op, cit., pp. 661f.

18  J. Lepore, op, cit., p. 187.

19  J. Charlton, *The Chartists*, London 1997, p. 34. Tellingly, the combative anti-democrat Lord Macaulay was later included in the capitalist canon peddled across the North Atlantic by the US Liberty Fund, established in 1960.

20  P. Foot, *The Vote*, London 2012, p. 95.

21  P. Foot, op. cit., p 116.

22  J. Charlton, *The Chartists*, London 1997, p. 15.

23  S. P. Huntington, *The Third Wave*, Norman, Oklahoma 1991, p. 6.

24  P. Foot, op. cit., pp. 103, 146 and 157, respectively.

25  The liberals feared a clerical-directed female vote. M. Liebman, *Les socialistes belges 1885–1914*, Brussels 1979, p. 133.

26  *Program vid rösträttsmöte 1890 I Lill-Jans*, 1890, p. 105.

27  J. Nehru, *India's Freedom*, London 1962/1936 pp. 21 and 32.

28  N. Mandela, *Long Walk to Freedom*, London 1995, p. 391.

29  B. Bréville, '"Quelle est votre race?"', *Le Monde Diplomatique*, July 2019, p. 12.

30  Conceptions of nation, people and citizenship in nineteenth-century Hispanic America are extensively treated in H. Sábato (ed.), *Ciudanía política y formación de naciones*, Mexico D.F. 1997; A. Annino and F-X. Guerra (eds), *Inventando la nación*, Mexico D.F. 2003; M.-D. Demélas, *La Invención Política*, Lima 2003 (original French edition Paris 1992)

31  F-X. Guerra, 'El soberano y su reino', in H. Sábato, op. cit., p. 44.

32  G. Freyre, *The Masters and the Slaves*, New York 1964, (original Brazilian edition 1933); J. Vasconcelos, *The Cosmic Race* (bilingual ed., original Mexican ed. 1929), Baltimore 1997.

33  *Dred Scott vs. Sandford*, at 403, here cited from wikipedia.org.

34  Martin Luther King, Jr., 'I Have a Dream' speech, available at archives.gov.

35  Malcolm X at the Audubon Ballroom, teachingamericanhistory. org/library.

36  R. P. Green Jr. and H. D. Cheatham (eds), *The American Civil Rights Movement: A Documentary History*, Manchester 2009, chapter 8.

37  See Elizabeth Cady Stanton, 'The Seneca Falls Declaration 1848', available at let.rug.nl/usa/documents/1826-1850/the-seneca-falls-declaration-1848.php.

38  R. Sharpe, *The Persons Case: The Origins and Legacy of the Fight for Legal Personhood*, Toronto 2007.

39  R. J. Evans, *The Feminists*, London 1979, p. 152.

40  See further my *Between Sex and Power: Family in the World, 1900–2000*, London 2004, pp. 102ff.

41  T. Iversen and D. Soskice, *Democracy and Prosperity*, Princeton 2019.

42  The meeting is portrayed by Éric Vuillard, *The Order of the Day*, London 2018, pp. 1–17. (The original edition, *L'ordre du jour*, Paris 2017, was awarded the Prix Goncourt.)

43  Here quoted from T. Piketty, *Capital et idéologie*, Paris 2019, p. 824n.

44  M. Crozier, S. Hungtington and J. Watanuki, *The Crisis of Democracy*, New York 1975. Quotes are from pp. 60 and 113 (Huntington), 11 (Crozier), and 161 (Conclusion). Watanuki gave a different diagnosis of Japan, more concerned with democracy than with governability. In Britain the Essex political scientist Anthony King is usually seen as another forerunner to elite concern with government 'overload': A. King, 'Overload Problems of Governing in the 1970s', *Political Studies*, 23/2–3 1975, p. 284.

45  Cf. M. Moran, 'What Happened to Overloaded Government?',

*Political Quarterly*, 89/1, 2018; A Przeworski, *Why Bother with Elections?*, Cambridge 2018, pp. 43ff, on 'Counter-Majoritarian Institutions'.

46  K. von Beyme, *Systemwechsel in Osteuropa*, Frankfurt 1994, pp. 100 and 114.

47  K. von Beyme, op. cit., p. 116.

48  T. Garton Ash, *The Magic Lantern*, New York 1990, pp. 42–3.

49  W. Miller et al., *Values and Political Change in Postcommunist Europe*, Basingstoke 1998, Tables 6.1–6.4. The 'market economy' received much better scores and majority support, when separated from the distinctive features of capitalism, private bosses, profit orientation in social services, abolition of job security and workers' rights, Table 6.1.

50  Ibid., Table 10.16.

51  M. Brost and M. Böick, 'Das abgeschriebene Land', *Die Zeit*, 2 October 2019, pp. 215–27.

52  Ibid., *Die Zeit*, 2 October 2019, p. 2.

53  P.C. Schmitter, '"Real-Existing" Democracy and its Discontents: Sources, Conditions, Causes, Symptoms, and Prospects', *Chinese Political Science Review*, 4/2, 2019.

54  J. Schumpeter, *Capitalism, Socialism and Democracy*, London 1943, chapter XXII.

55  Huntington, op. cit., p. 6.

56  A. Przeworski, et al., *Democracy and Development*, Cambridge 2000, pp. 27ff.

57  L. Bartels, *Unequal Democracy*, Princeton 2008 (1st ed.) and 2016 (2nd ed.), M. Giles, *Affluence and Influence*, Princeton 2012.

58  L. Bartels, op. cit., (2nd ed.), pp. 242ff.

59  M. Giles, op. cit., p. 82.

60  'Who Got What They Wanted? The Opinion-Policy Link in Sweden, 1956–2014', Gothenburg University, Department of Political Science, 2017, pp. 16–19.

61  Oral communication at a dinner in Istanbul a few years ago.

62  A. Tooze, '"Cruelly absent grandeur"?', *Geschichte und Gesellschaft*, vol. 44 (2018), p. 466.

63  'Poverty in the UK is "Systematic" and "Tragic" says UN Special Rapporteur', *BBC*, 22 May 2019, bbc.co.uk; R. Booth, 'UN Report Compares Tory Welfare Policies to Creation of Workhouses', *The Guardian*, 22 May 2019.

64  Child poverty is here defined as children in households with no more than 60 per cent of the median income of the nation: Luxemburg Income Study, *Key Figures*, lisdatacenter.org.

65  Kayleigh Garthwaite, *Hunger Pains*, Bristol 2016, pp. 2ff and passim.

66  M. Gómez Garrido, et al., 'The Role of Grassroots Food Banks in Building Political Solidarity with Vulnerable People', *European Societies*, 21/3, pp. 753–73, 2018.
67  Oral communication; D. Goffart, *Das Ende der Mittelschicht*, Berlin 2019, p. 213.
68  R. Wuthnow, *The Left Behind*, Princeton 2018.
69  Eurostat, *Urban Europe 2016*, p. 78.
70  Office for National Statistics, *Avoidable Mortality in the UK: 2017*.
71  E. Nosrati, *The Political Economy of Life and Death in the USA*, PhD Thesis, Department of Sociology, University of Cambridge 2018, Figure 6.5.
72  K. D. Kochanek, et al., 'Mortality in the United States, 2016', *NCHS Data Brief*, no. 293, Washington, D.C. 2017, p. 3. See further A. Case and A. Deaton, *Deaths of Despair*, Princeton 2020
73  Statistics Sweden, *Förväntad medellivslängd, 2013–2017 jämfört med 2008–2012*.
74  F. Alvaredo, et al, *World Inequality Report 2018*, Figure 2.4.8.
75  On Sweden, see further my 'Sweden's Turn to Inequality, 1982–2019', *Structural Change and Economic Dynamics*, Vol 52, March 2020, pp. 159–166. On Germany, O. Nachtwey, *Germany's Hidden Crisis: Social Decline in the Heart of Europe*, London 2018.
76  T. Piketty, *Capital et idéologie*, op cit., p. 617. Redistribution is measured in terms of the ratio of the average income of the top 10 and the bottom 50 per cent of the population, before and after taxes and transfers.
77  On the Southern literature, see for example *The Economist*, 'Burgeoning Bourgeoisie', special report, 14 February 2009; H. Kharas, ' The Emerging Middle Class in Developing Countries', Working paper, OECD Development Centre 2010; H. Melber (ed.), *The Rise of Africa's Middle Class*, London 2016; Asia Development Bank, 'The Rise of Asia's Middle Class', in idem, *Key Indicators for Asia and the Pacific 2010, Manila 2011*, J. Dayton-Johnson (ed.), *Latin America's Emerging Middle Classes*, London 2015 Some of the Northern literature will be considered below.
78  T. Iversen and D. Soskice, *Democracy and Prosperity*, op. cit., pp. 20, 21 and 25.
79  D. Boyle, *Broke*, London 2014. D. Goffart, *Das Ende der Mittelschicht*, Berlin 2019; C. Guilluy, *No society. La fin de la classe moyenne occidentale*, Paris 2018; P. Temin, *The Vanishing Middle Class*, Cambridge MA, 2017; L. Chauvel, *Les classes moyennes à la dérive*, Paris 2016.
80  J. C. Gornick and M. Jäntti (eds), *Income Inequality: Economic Disparities and the Middle Class in Affluent Countries*,

Stanford 2013; D. Markovits, *The Meritocracy Trap*, London 2019; T. Piketty, *Capital et idéologie*, op. cit., pp. 609ff.

81 T. Blanchet, et al., 'How Unequal is Europe? Evidence from Distributional National Accounts, 1980–2017', World Inequality Database, wid.world, table 1.

82 High Pay Centre, 'Executive Pay in the FTSE 100', 2018 and 2019 reports at highpaycentre.org.

83 High Pay Centre, 'One Law for Them', 2016, highpaycentre.org, p. 4.

84 US Department of Commerce, Economics and Statistics Administration, 'Middle Class in America', 2010, p. 1, commerce.gov

85 R. Chetty et al., 'The Fading American Dream: Trends in Absolute Income Mobility since 1940', NBER Working Paper 22910, 2016.

86 L. Chauvel, 'Welfare Regimes, Cohorts, and the Middle Classes', pp. 114–41 in J.C. Gornick and M. Jäntti (eds), *Income Inequality: Economic Disparities and the Middle Class in Affluent Countries*, Stanford 2013, p. 133. See further idem, *Les classes moyennes à la dérive*, Paris 2016.

87 OECD, *Under Pressure: The Squeezed Middle Class*, Paris 2019, oecd.org, p. 26

88 OECD, *A Broken Social Elevator? How to Promote Social Mobility*, Paris 2018, oecd.org, pp. 251, 119, and 114f, respectively.

89 OECD, op. cit., p. 24.

90 P. Temin, *The Vanishing Class*, Cambridge MA 2017, p. 43.

91 E. Warren, *This Fight is our Fight*, New York 2018, p. 30.

92 See the goals set in the *Annual Report of the White House Task Force on the Middle Class*, 2010, obamawhitehouse.archives.gov; on the Department of Commerce, see n83 above.

93 'Home Ownership in England at a 30-year low', *The Guardian*, 2 March 2017. Among households in England, home ownership declined from 74 per cent in 2003-4 to 66 per cent in 2017–18, DCLG, *English Housing Survey 2017–18*.

94 D. Markovits, *The Meritocracy Trap*, New York 2019, p. 26, and appendix Tables 1 and 2.

95 Stanford Center on Poverty and Inequality, 'Income Segregation in the United States' Largest Metropolitan Areas', stanford.edu, Stand 2009.

96 S.F. Reardon and K. Bischoff, 'The Continuing Increase in Income Segregation, 2007–12', Stanford Center on Poverty and Inequality 2016, stanford.edu, Table 1.

97 T. Travers, et al., *Housing and Inequality in London*, Centre for London, April 2016, centreforlondon.org, figure 2.1, and p. 39, respectively.

98 Ministry of Housing, Communities, and Local Government, 'English

Housing Survey 2017–18', Annex Table 1.2. gov.uk/government/collections/english-housing-survey#2017-to-2018.

99  See my article 'Sweden's Turn to Inequality, 1982–2019', in *Structural Change and Economic Development*, 52, March 2020, pp. 159–166.

100  S. Musterd, et al., 'Socioeconomic Segregation in European Capital Cities. Increasing Separation between Poor and Rich', *Urban Geography*, 38/7, 1062–83, Figures 1–2, pp. 1074f.

101  J. Cribb, et al., 'Who are Business Owners and What are they Doing', Institute for Fiscal Studies, 9 July 2019, ifs.org.uk

102  D. Boyle, *How to Survive the Middle-Class Crisis*, London 2014, p. 248.

103  The literature on the contemporary crisis of democracy is vast. Two major recent contributions are W. Merkel (ed.), *Democracy and Crisis*, Cham, Switzerland 2018, (original German edition 2015) and A. Przeworski, *Crisis of Democracy*, Cambridge 2019.

104  R. Heede, 'Tracing Anthropogenic Carbon Dioxide and Methane Emissions to Fossil Fuel and Cement Producers, 1854–2010', *Climate Change*, 122, 2014, pp. 229–41 and p. 237.

105  L. Chancel and T. Piketty, *Carbon and Inequality: From Kyoto to Paris*, Paris School of Economics, November 2015, p. 9.

106  A. B. Atkinson and T. Piketty (eds), *Top Incomes: A Global Perspective*, Oxford 2010. Piketty, *Capital in the Twenty-First Century*, Cambridge MA 2014; *Capital et idéologie*, Paris 2019; E. Saez and G. Zucman, *The Triumph of Injustice*, New York 2019; G. Zucman, *The Hidden Wealth of Nations*, Chicago 2015. Piketty is also the central figure of the World Inequality Database being built, from which F. Alvaredo, et al., *World Inequality Report 2018*, stems.

107  B. Milanović, *Global Inequality*, Cambridge MA 2016; *Capitalism Alone*, Cambridge MA 2019; J. Stiglitz, *The Price of Inequality*, New York 2012.

108  A. Banerjee and E. Duflo, *Good Economics for Hard Times*, London 2019, p. 326.

109  R. Wilkinson and K. Pickett, *The Spirit Level*, London 2009; *The Inner Level*, London 2018; D. Dorling, *Injustice*, Bristol 2010 (second edition, 2015), *Inequality and the 1%*, London 2014.

110  B. Markovits, *The Meritocracy Trap*, op. cit.; E. Saez and G. Zucman, *The Triumph of Injustice*, op. cit.; T. Piketty, *Capital et idéologie*, op. cit., p. 1190.

111  Z. Sternhell, *The Anti-Enlightenment Tradition*, New Haven 2009.

112  *Economist*, 30 November 2019, Leader, p. 11–12.

113  www.medicinenet.com

114  A. Case and A. Deaton, Deaths of Despair, Princeton 2020, p. 145.
115  E. Saez and G. Zucman, The Triumph of Injustice, op. cit., pp. 82 and 14.
116  L. Chancel and T. Piketty, Carbon and Inequality: From Kyoto to Paris, op. cit., p. 33.
117  The richest Dutch and Swedish citizens took 53 per cent of household income during the WWI speculative boom in the two neutral countries, and Brazilians 55 per cent in 2015. American, Dutch and Swedish figures are from A. B. Atkinson and T. Piketty (eds), Top Incomes in Global Perspective, op. cit., pp. 716, 725 and 739, respectively. The Brazilian from F. Alavaredo, et al., World Inequality Report 2018, p. 43.
118  World Bank data. Gini coefficients are never quite stable.
119  W. Scheidel, The Great Leveller, Princeton 2017.
120  Market income inequality reduction 2015 from Eurostat. Growth data from A. Maddison, Contours of the World Economy, 1–2030 AD, Oxford 2007, Table A5. Average annual economic growth in developed Western Europe 1950–1973 was 4.65 per cent, the US was 3.93 – rates which the North Atlantic economic region has not been close to since the inegalitarian turn in 1980.
121  The relatively egalitarian Nordic countries are regularly ranked among the world's ten to fifteen most competitive countries.
122  International Labour Organization (ILO), 'Status in Employment', ilostat.ilo.org, 2018; UNCTAD, Trade and Development Report 2016; Dani Rodrik, 'Premature Deindustrialisation', NBER Working Paper 20935, (2015).
123  T. Piketty, Capital et idéologie, op. cit., pp. 978f.
124  With the wisdom of hindsight, one might say that the least bad option for the Labour leadership would have been to let through Johnson's EU deal with a free party vote. Then the debate on the future society of Britain could have started.
125  C. Crouch, Post-Democracy, Cambridge 2004, p. 123,
126  ILO Monitor, COVID-19 and the World of Work, third ed., p. 2, www.ilo.org.
127  M. Talev, 'Axios-Ipsos Coronavirus Index: Rich sheltered, poor shafted amid virus', accessed at axios.com/axios-ipsos-coronavirus-index-rich-sheltered-poor-shafted-9e592100-b8e6-4dcd-aeeo-a6516892874b.html. The index was followed up 21 April.
128  Al Jazeera 1 April 2020.
129  P. Wintour, 'El nuevo orden mundial tras el coronavirus: el debate soterrano de la geopolítica ya ha empezado', desde abajo (Colombia) 14 April 2020.

130 US and India, K.P. Kannan, 'COVID-19 Lockdown', *Economic and Political Weekly*, 3 April 2020; 'Italy ups coronavirus stimulus spending to 370 billion euros – nearly half of GDP', *Euronews* 7 April 2020.

131 A. Nussbaum and P. Donahue, 'Germany and France Blame Americans for Playing Dirty Over Masks', *Bloomberg*, 3 April 2020.

132 According to the COVID-19 tracker at worldometers.info/coronavirus, accessed 1 July 2020.

## 2. The Rule of Capital and the Rise of Democracy

1 J. S. Mill, 'Considerations on Representative Government', in *On Liberty and Considerations on Representative Government*, Oxford 1946, pp. 217ff.

2 For the problem of the class character of the state power apparatus, see Göran Therborn, *What Does the Ruling Class Do When It Rules?*, London 1978, Part One.

3 These important aspects of democracy are not explicitly considered here. For a very good survey of the position in the major Western countries, see F. Castberg, *Freedom of Speech in the West*, Oslo and London 1960.

4 Post-war Japan provides an instance of significant overweighting of the rural electorate, the purpose of which was to install the right-wing Liberals in power in 1949 (with 264 out of 466 seats elected by 43.8 per cent of voters) and to keep them there in the sixties and seventies. J. A. A. Stockwin, *Japan: Divided Politics in a Growth Economy*, London 1975, pp. 55, 91ff.

5 The political system which followed Louis Napoleon's 18 Brumaire is the subject of an exquisite work of historical scholarship: T. Zeldin, *The Political System of Napoleon III*, London 1958. For information on the Giolitti regime I have relied heavily on G. Carocci, *Giolitti e l'età giolittiana*, Turin 1961.

6 B. K. Garis, '1890–1900', in F. Crowley (ed.), *A New History of Australia*, Melbourne 1974, pp. 242–3.

7 In 1901 there were 40,000 Asians in Australia out of a population of 3,750,000. See A. T. Yarwood, *Asian Migration to Australia*, Melbourne 1964, p. 163.

8 G. D. H. Cole, *A History of Socialist Thought*, Vol. III, part 2, London 1956, pp. 621ff.

9 V. Lorwin, 'Belgium', in R. Dahl (ed.), *Political Oppositions in Western Democracies*, New Haven and London 1966, p. 158.

10  D. Sternberger and B. Vogel (eds), *Die Wahl der Parlamente und anderer Staatsorgane*, Berlin 1969, vol. 1, p. 93.

11  Ibid., pp. 119–20.

12  A thrilling insight into official Canadian anti-communism may be gained from a booklet published by the Royal Canadian Mounted Police: *Law and Order in Canadian Democracy*, Ottawa 1952, chapters 12 and 13.

13  In Denmark and Norway the liberal party called itself Left, opposed to the conservative Right, and has kept the label into the twenty-first century.

14  S. Nordenstreng, *L. Mechelin*, vol. II, Helsinki 1937, p. 334. Mechelin was by that time the leading politician in Finland.

15  Ibid., pp. 386ff.

16  J-P. Charnay, *Le suffrage politique en France*, Paris 1965, pp. 143–75.

17  The evaluation of the 1919 elections is based on C. Seton-Watson, *Italy from Liberalism to Fascism, 1870–1925*, London 1967, p. 547.

18  J. Maki, *Government and Politics in Japan*, London 1962, pp. 78ff.

19  For an overview in English, see E. H. Kossman, *The Low Countries, 1780–1940*, Oxford 1978, pp. 85ff, 359ff, 554ff.

20  W. H. Oliver, *The Story of New Zealand*, London 1960, p. 157; P. Grimshaw, *Women's Suffrage in New Zealand*, Auckland 1972. The main feminist organization was the Women's Christian Temperance Union.

21  The national background to the inclusion of universal male suffrage in the Left party programme is clear from the official party history. See J. Worm-Müller, et al., *Venstre i Norge*, Oslo 1933, pp. 124ff.

22  G. Gerdner, *Ministären Edèn och författningsrevisionen*, Uppsala 1944.

23  V. Gitermann, *Geschichte der Schweiz*, Thayngen-Schaffhausen 1941, pp. 510ff.

24  E. Gruner, *Die Parteien in der Schweiz*, Berne 1969, p. 181.

25  J. Sigler, *American Rights Policies*, Homewood, IL 1975, pp. 113–14.

26  This has been convincingly argued, on the basis of solid research, by M. Kousser, op. cit.

27  A. Holcombe, *State Government in the United States*, New York 1916, p. 149.

28  W. D. Burnham, 'The United States', in R. Rose (ed.), *Electoral Behaviour*, op. cit., p. 677.

29  P. Vigier, *La Seconde République*, Paris 1967, pp. 76f.

30  For a monograph on the history of the 1919 constitution, see S. Lindman, *Från storfurstendöme till republik*, Ekenäs 1969.

31 G.-H. Dumont, *Histoire de la Belgique*, vol. III, Brussels 1956, p. 192. The mutinous departure of German troops from Brussels led to a popular upsurge, involving strikes and a hunt for collaborators; ruling-class fear of revolution haunted the obscure and complex round of negotiations at the castle of Loppem that resulted in the king's speech. It is uncertain whether, in the absence of this fear, a decisive section of the Catholic political establishment would have rebelled against the eighty-year-old reactionary diehard, Woeste, and rallied to the support of bourgeois democracy. See C.-H. Höjer, *Le régime parlementaire belge de 1918 à 1940*, Uppsala 1946, chapter 3.

32 T. Hamerow, *The Social Foundations of German Unification Struggles and Accomplishments*, Princeton 1972, p. 244.

33 M. Weiss, *Die Ausbreitung des allgemeinen und gleichen, parlamentarischen Wahlrechts in der westlichen Reichshälfte der Habsburgmonarchie*, Heidelberg 1965, pp. 248ff.

34 Towards the end of 1918, representatives of the engineering industry and the main banks demanded that the right-wing leaders accept democratization. See S. A. Söderpalm, *Storföretagarna och det demokratiska genombrottet*, Lund 1969, pp. 174ff. Söderpalm does not go into the social roots of these politicians. However, all three of them – Lindman, Trygger and Swartz – were connected, either by family or profession, with the traditional wood and iron combines (Lindman had been the chief executive of one of them). The division of German monopoly capital between coal-iron and electro-chemical interests was developed into an instrument of historical analysis by the great East German historian Jürgen Kuczynski. To my knowledge the finest use of it has been made by another GDR historian, Kurt Gossweiler, in *Grossbanken, Industrienmonopole, Staat*, Berlin 1971. The Belgian financier Émile Francqui also seems to have played an important pro-democratic role within the cabal that lay behind the king's speech of 22 November 1918. See Höjer, op. cit., pp. 64, 82–3.

35 F. Dovring, *Land and Labor in Europe in the Twentieth Century*, The Hague 1965, p. 169. As a result of the successful co-operative activities of the Boerenbond (which was a junior member of the Catholic electoral cartel), Belgian tenant-farmers had few import and macroeconomic conflicts with their landlords.

36 R. Blake, *Disraeli*, London 1966, chapter XXI. The account contains a striking picture of Disraeli setting his secretaries to work, under extreme time pressure and with the aid of crude savings-bank and tax records, to calculate the electoral consequences to the Tories and Liberals of various suffrage qualifications.

37 H. Zwager, *De motivering van het algemeen kiesrecht in Europa*,

Groningen 1958, pp. 161ff; A. Lijphart, *The Politics of Accommodation*, Berkeley and Los Angeles 1968, pp. 104ff.

38  Quoted from W. Gillette, *The Right to Vote*, Baltimore 1965, p. 164. Gillette has conclusively uncovered the political context of the passing of the Fifteenth Amendment.

39  In Japan, not even crushing military defeat was sufficient to dislocate the power bloc constituted by monopoly capital and the late-feudal imperial state bureaucracy. As Baron Shidehara's government could not bring itself to accept unequivocally popular sovereignty, the American occupation command stepped in to draft a democratic constitution. The resoluteness shown by the US government, so different from its attitude at home, should be seen primarily as an attempt to eradicate the social roots of Japanese imperialism, which had in the past posed a deadly threat to American world interests. When communism once more became the main enemy, the fate of Japanese democracy no longer seemed that important. Thus, a workers' strike was banned as early as 1947 (Stockwin, op. cit., p. 56) and the Americans co-operated quite closely with Nobusuke Kishi – a former member of General Tojo's war cabinet and a convicted war criminal (ibid. p. 60) – when he became prime minister in 1957. It was as if Albert Speer had gone straight from Spandau to the federal chancellery in Bonn.

40  In *A Century of Pay* (London 1968, p. 312), E. H. Phelps Brown and M. H. Browne have shown that during most of the period from 1895 to 1960, the ratio of average annual wages per wage-earner to average annual income generated per person occupied in industry fell in the US, the UK, Germany and Sweden; but that real wages rose because of increases in productivity.

41  These mechanisms are touched on in *What Does the Ruling Class Do When It Rules?*, op. cit.

42  Norway provides an example of such effects produced by the commercialization of agriculture. See O. Osterud, 'The Transformation of Scandinavian Agrarianism', *Scandinavian Journal of History*, vol 1, 1976, pp. 201–13.

43  J.R. Pole's *Political Representation in England and the Origins of the American Republic* (London 1966) is a solid and interesting study of the rise of the individual right to political representation.

44  G. D. H. Cole, op. cit., p. 876.

45  This is argued in, amongst other works, D. Sternberger and B. Vogel, op. cit., pp. 1127f.

46  True, there were more defeats than victories – thirty-two to nine between 1869 and 1916. See A. S. Kraditor, *The Ideas of the Woman Suffrage Movement: 1890–1920*, New York 1966, p. 5.

47  Ibid., p. 231.

48  F. Crowley, op. cit., p. 241.

49  H. Clodie, *Canadian Government and Politics*, Toronto 1944, p. 102.

50  J. Bryce, *The American Commonwealth*, New York 1911, vol. II, p. 687.

51  N. G. Butlin, 'Some Perspectives of Australian Economic Development 1890–1965', in C. Forster (ed.), *Australian Economic Development in the Twentieth Century*, London and Sydney 1970, p. 274.

52  This correlation does not apply at all in the case of Utah, which had an approximately even sex distribution. See A. Grimes, *The Puritan Ethic and Woman Suffrage*, New York 1967, p. xi.

53  A. Raeburn, *The Militant Suffragettes* (Swedish edition), Stockholm 1975, p. 11. American women had the support not only of the small socialist movement but even of Gompers and the AFL (see D. Morgan, *Suffragists and Democrats*, East Lansing 1972). Morgan has also written a monograph on the contradictory relationship between the British Liberal Party and the women's movement: *Suffragists and Liberals*, Oxford 1975.

54  E. Håstad, *Regeringssättet i den schweiziska demokratin*, Uppsala and Stockholm 1936, p. 262n. This 700-page Swedish treatise on Swiss democratic government is representative of the general indulgence towards Swiss sexism. Thus, while it deals with the ceremonies and festivities usually accompanying elections, it contains no discussion at all of the reasons for the exclusion of women. The contemporary Swiss writer Gruner is equally unconcerned.

55  J. Bryce, op. cit., vol. II, p. 604.

56  The need for allies, and the crucial role of rural populism and of the agricultural proletariat (which at first largely determined the strength of the labour movement) explain the perhaps surprising fact that the breakthroughs in female enfranchisement came not in the industrial, political and cultural centres of the world (such as London, Manchester, Paris, Berlin, Rome, Milan, New York, Chicago, Montreal, Melbourne or Sydney) but in peripheral rural areas like New Zealand, Southern and Western Australia, Finland, Norway, and the western states and provinces of the US and Canada.

57  A partial exception were the patriarchal and polygamous Mormon settlers of Utah, who gave their women the vote in order to blunt outside criticism and to fend off unbelievers – in particular the young bachelor miners brought in by the transcontinental railway. See Grimes, op. cit., chapter 2.

58  For France see M. Duverger, *Droit constitutionnel et institutions politiques*, Paris 1959, vol. I, p. 87. However, Duverger

unreservedly accepts the explanation of the Swiss case by the institution of male referenda. Campbell, op. cit., p. 102. The Belgian Liberals adamantly opposed the female vote in 1919, while the Social Democrats, who secured its introduction in municipal elections, agreed to postpone it for national ones. (Höjer, op. cit., pp. 95–6.) A survey of Swiss developments up to 1958 is provided by two articles in *Revue française de Science politique*: A. Quinche, 'Le suffrage féminin en Suisse'; J.-F. Aubert, 'Le suffrage féminin en Suisse', in vols. 4 and 8 (1954, 1958) respectively, as well as by the official report of the Federal Council on women's suffrage – *Bundesblatt*, 109/10, Berne 1957. According to the latter, the female population of Berne canton obtained a restricted vote during the radical movement of the 1830s, but was deprived of it by the cantonal government in 1887 (p. 691). *Keesing's Contemporary Archives* contains reports of the 1959 and 1971 referenda, and of the 1971 parliamentary decision. The last outpost of Swiss political sexism seems to have been the small rural, German-speaking Catholic cantons, while Protestant Zurich and Catholic Lucerne were of decisive pro-democratic importance in 1971. My hypothesis of the role of bourgeois anti-clericalism finds little direct confirmation in the above surveys – it would appear that where anti-clericalism is more of a proletarian than a bourgeois current, it serves as no obstacle to the achievement of women's rights.

59 G. Ionescu and I. de Madariaga, *Opposition*, Harmondsworth 1972, chapter 2.

## 3. The Right to Vote and the Four World Routes to/through Modernity

1 G. Therborn, 'The Rule of Capital and the Rise of Democracy', *New Left Review*, I/103, May–June 1977, included in this volume; 'The Travail of Latin American Democracy', *New Left Review*, I/113, January–April 1979.

2 My first attempt was 'Vías a través la modernidad', a lecture to the Mexican Congress, published in *Relaciones* 4, Mexico City 1990. Later developed in, inter alia, *The World*, Cambridge 2011, pp. 54–83.

3 The four routes to and through modernity can be situated in a two-dimensional framework. One dimension, then, is the location of the Old Order, internally to the area or externally. The external Old Order separates the New Worlds from the rest. The other axis is the location of the forces of modernization. In Europe, the latter

were clearly internal. With some qualifications the same holds for the New Worlds. In the Colonial Zone, modernity clearly came from abroad. In between is the case of externally induced, but internally initiated and led, modernization.

4   A. Marongiu, *Medieval Parliaments*, London 1968; cf. O. Hintze, *The Historical Essays of Otto Hintze*, New York 1975, chapter 8.

5   L. Schnorr von Carolsfeld, 'Representatio – Eine Untersuchung über den Gebrauch dieses Ausdrucks in der römischen Literatur', in H. Rausch (ed.), *Die geschichtlichen Grundlagen der modernen Volksvertretung*, Darmstadt 1980; A. Marongiu, op. cit., pp. 35ff; idem, 'Das Prinzip der Demokratie und der Zustimmung ... im 14. Jahrhundert', in H. Rausch, op. cit.; Y. Congar, 'Quod omnes tangit, ab omnibus tractari et approbari debet', in H. Rausch, op. cit.

6   K. von Beyme, 'Representatives under parlamentarisches Regierungssystem', in H. Rausch, op. cit.

7   Cf. P. Anderson, *Lineages of the Absolutist State*, London 1974.

8   Only between 25 and 30 per cent of the citizens of Athens could be seated in the assembly in the Pnyx in the fourth century BC: J. Ober, *Mass and Elite in Democratic Athens*, Princeton 1989, pp. 28n, 132.

9   The first constitution of the French Revolution, in 1791, explicitly excluded wage-workers from the electorate: D. Sternberger and B. Vogel, op. cit., p. 444.

10  W. Bagehot, *The English Constitution*, London 1964/1867, pp. 162 and 277, respectively.

11  F. Furet and M. Ozouf (eds), *Dictionnaire critique de la Révolution française*, Paris 1988, p. 66.

12  His coup was blessed by 92 per cent of the 80 per cent who fulfilled their duty to vote: P. Stearns, *1848: The Revolutionary Tide in Europe*, New York 1974, p. 222. In the parliamentary elections His New Imperial Majesty's government managed to get 89.1 per cent of the vote in 1857, 74.2 per cent in 1863 and 55.0 per cent in 1869.

13  E. Ochoa, 'The Rapid Expansion of Voter Participation in Latin American Presidential Elections, 1845–1986', in J. Wilke and D. Lorey (eds), *Statistical Abstract of Latin America*, vol. 27, Los Angeles 1989.

14  D. Sternberger and B. Vogel, op. cit., p. 211.

15  Among the UK population, 28.8 per cent of those twenty years and older had the right to vote: D. Sternberger and B. Vogel, op. cit.

16  A. Mayer, *The Persistence of the Old Regime*, London 1981.

17  F. O'Gorman, *Patrons and Parties: The Unreformed Electoral System of Hanoverian England, 1734–1832*, Oxford 1989.

18  M. Dogan, 'Romania 1919–1938', in M. Weiner and E. Özbudun (eds), *Competitive Elections in Developing Countries*, Durham NC 1978.

19  The 'council movement' dated back to the Russian upheavals in 1905. It had interesting connections with official institutional models, such as the 1903 legislation on 'factory aldermen' elected among the workers, and the provision of the elections of delegates to a short-lived governmental commission of investigation into 'the causes of the dissatisfaction of the Petersburg factory workers' (Anweiler, 1958: 43ff.). The provisions of the Tsarist five-curiae electoral order of 1907 involved a pyramid of indirect elections by class, elections which for workers were not territorial but by workplace and industry: D. Sternberger and B. Vogel, op. cit., pp. 1157–77.

20  M. Ferro, *La Révolution de 1917*, vol. 1, Paris 1967, p. 452.

21  O. Anweiler, *Die Rätebewegung in Russland, 1905–1921*, Leiden 1958 pp. 152ff.

22  Cited by G. Ritter and A. Müller (eds), *Die deutsche Revolution, 1918-19*, Frankfurt 1968, p. 110.

23  Cf. W. Wefers, *Grundlagen und Ideen des spanischen Staates der Gegenwart*, Bonn 1961; E. Tálos and W. Neugebauer (eds), '*Austrofascismus*', Vienna 1984.

24  Bernard Bailyn in his *The Origins of American Politics* (New York 1970) has highlighted, for British North America, the explosive potential of representative assemblies, fed by the radical culture in the wake of the Glorious Revolution, without the old social and political order that ensured stable rule in England.

   Section 6 of the pioneering declaration the Virginia Bill of Rights (of 12 June 1776) began thus: 'That elections of members to serve as representatives of the people, in assembly, ought to be free; and that all men, having sufficient evidence of permanent common interest with and attachment to the community, have the right of suffrage' (here quoted from the documentation compiled by F. Hartung, *Die Entwicklung der Menschen- und Bürgerrechte von 1776 bis zur Gegenwart*, Göttingen 1964, p. 38).

25  For colonial and post-colonial suffrage in the United States I am mainly relying on Clinton Williamson's investigation, *American Suffrage: From Property to Democracy, 1760–1860*, Princeton 1960.

26  C. Williamson, op. cit., p. 38.

27  The importance of this is underlined by the violent constitutional conflict of the 1840s, the 'Dorr War', in Rhode Island, where a relatively large non-WASP proletariat had emerged (see, for example, C. Wlliamson, op. cit., p. 268). Contrast this with the smoothness

of New York City development in S. Wilentz, *Chants Democratic: New York City and the Rise of the American Working Class, 1788–1850*, Oxford 1984.

28  P. Bairoch, *The Working Population and Its Structure*, Brussels 1968, Table A2. See further, G. Therborn, *European Modernity and Beyond*, London 1995, pp. 65ff.

29  Restrictions varied. Some property or income qualification was very common, sometimes wage-earners were excluded, sometimes literacy requirements were invoked, which hit widely. The defeat of the first revolutionary wave led to widespread doubts about representative government and republicanism, not least in the Liberator himself, Simón Bolívar. The source of my conclusions on early Latin American constitutions is the five-volume documentation *El pensamiento constitucional hispanoamericano hasta 1830*, Caracas 1961. I have also used the later collection of constitutions edited by R. Fitzgibbon, *The Constitution of the Americas*, Chicago 1968. See further the context in J. Lynch, *The Spanish American Revolutions, 1808–1826*, New York 1975.

30  So called after the 'Reform banquets' which led up to the French February Revolution of 1848, the demand of which went back to the British Parliamentary Reform Act of 1832. See further, J. Covo, *Les idées de la 'Reforma' au Méxique, 1855–1861*, 2 volumes, New Haven CT 1982; and J. F. Leal and J. Woldenberg, *Del estado liberal a los inicios de la dictadura porfirista*, Mexico City 1980.

31  In Chile before 1964 at most 16.9 per cent of the population participated in a presidential election (Ochoa, op. cit., p. 87). In Argentina before 1916 and in Brazil until the 1930s, only between 2 and 3 per cent of the population voted. In 1945, Brazilian participation went up to 13.4 per cent, and Argentina's leaped from 17.2 per cent in the first Perón election of 1945 to 42.3 per cent in the second half of 1951. How many people participated in the first stage of the indirect Mexican elections under the 1857 constitution is unknown, but after the Revolution, participation stayed around 10 to 12 per cent until 1958. In the US, the lowest electoral turnout after 1848 was in 1864, at 11.9 per cent, and in 1920, with female suffrage, participation went from 18.4 to 25.1 per cent of the population (Ochoa, op. cit., pp. 160ff). In France, by comparison, the electoral turnout comprised of 19 per cent of the population in 1848 and passed 20 per cent in the very beginning of the Third Republic, in 1877. In 1945, electoral participation jumped to 48 per cent, from 22 per cent in 1936 (Sternberger and Vogel, op. cit., pp. 160ff). In British parliamentary elections, more than 10 per cent of the population voted by 1885 and 25 per cent in 1918 (P. Flora (ed.), *State, Economy and Society in Western*

*Europe, 1815–1975*, 2 volumes, Frankfurt 1983 and 1987, vol. 1, p. 130, vol. 2, pp. 80ff). The first elections to the German Wilhelmine Diet in 1871 attracted 10 per cent of the population, the last in 1912 almost 19 per cent, and 48 per cent participated in the 1919 elections of the Weimar Republic (Sternberger and Vogel, op. cit., pp. 352ff). In the more politically open countries of Eastern Europe, Greece had since the 1880s a total of voters amounting to 10 per cent of the population, in 1963 ascending to 20 per cent. Bulgarian voters comprised 9 to 12 per cent of the population in the seven parliamentary elections from 1901 to the outbreak of the First World War, and constituted about 20 per cent in the 1920s elections (Sternberger and Vogel, op. cit., pp. 566 and 169, respectively).

32  The demarcation between the settler states of the New Worlds and the countries emerging from twentieth-century decolonization is precisely there. The line has been a front of bitter war. Rhodesia tried to create itself as another little New World, but failed and became an ex-colony, with special settler rights. South Africa has managed since 1910 as a New World, for many decades with increasingly intransigent racism. This racism came to constitute a colonial oppression of its own, for which the bell now tolls in the 1990s.

33  J. Lynch, op. cit., pp. 28f.

34  See further on this point and in general on ethnic relations in Spanish America at the time, R. Blackburn, *The Overthrow of Colonial Slavery*, London 1988, chapter 9.

35  His 'Angostura Speech' of 1819 to the Congress of Venezuela: S. Bolívar, *The Hope of the Universe*, Paris UNESCO 1983, p. 141. Bolívar's army contained high-ranking mulatto officers, and the great Mexican president elected in the late 1860s and early 1870s, Benito Juárez, was Indian.

36  C. Williamson, op. cit., p. 278.

37  M. Kousser, *The Shaping of Southern Politics*, New Haven CT 1974; P. Kleppner, *Who Voted?*, New York 1982.

38  P. Kleppner, op. cit.; F. Fox Piven and R. Cloward, *Why Americans Still Don't Vote*, New York 1988.

39  A. Borón, *The Formation and Crisis of the Liberal State in Argentina, 1880–1930*, Cambridge MA, Harvard PhD thesis, 1976, p. 176.

40  An important source for the following is G. Keaton (ed.), *The British Commonwealth: The Development of Its Laws and Constitutions*, volumes 5–14, London 1960–7. Further, I have been helped by H. Van Dorn, *Selected Constitutions of East Asia*, Kent OH, 1958, by the three volumes available to me of *Corpus*

*Constitutionnel* (1965–8), and by D. Nohlen, *Wahlsysteme der Welt*, Munich 1978. On French Black Africa I have made the most use of a couple of treatises in German: F. Ansprenger, *Politik im schwarzen Afrika*, Cologne 1961 and E. Fehr, *Demokratische Staatsformen in Westafrika*, Zürich 1965. Apart from works on individual colonies and nations, I have also a particular indebtedness to L. Diamond, et al., (eds), *Democracy in Developing Countries*, volumes on Africa and Asia, Boulder CO 1988 and 1989, and to R. B. Collier, *Regimes in Tropical Africa*, Berkeley 1982.

41  R. B. Collier, op. cit., pp. 42ff.

42  R. Lemarchand, *Rwanda and Burundi*, London 1970, pp. 81f. Portugal, before its entry into the United Nations, in 1951 officially incorporated its colonies as ordinary provinces. Somewhere around 0.1 to 0.2 per cent of the African population of these provinces then obtained citizenship rights as 'asimilados': P. Anderson, 'Portugal and the End of Ultra-Colonialism', *New Left Review* I/16, July–August 1962, p. 109.

43  J. McLane, *Indian Nationalism and the Early Congress*, Princeton 1977.

44  S. Sarkar, *Modern India, 1885–1947*, second edition, Basingstoke 1989, p. 67.

45  Government of India Act, 1935. First Schedule, paragraphs 18–23, available at legislation.gov.uk/ukpga/1935/2/pdfs/ukpga_19350002 _en.pdf.

46  K. M. De Silva, *A History of Sri Lanka*, London 1981, chapter 30.

47  Anti-Japanese in Burma, Malaya and Indochina; basically pro-Japanese in Indonesia; both in the Philippines; mainly neutral but in part pro-Japanese in India.

48  R. B. Collier, op. cit., pp. 50f.

49  Already before that, after the sudden riots in Leopoldville in early January 1959, the Belgians had given up.

50  Guinea voted for independence, and in Niger there was at least a fight, which the nationalists lost, by 22 to 78. In ten of the territories, the Frenchified African leaders, their impressively organized party, the colonial administration and the chiefs cooperated in bringing out the pro-French vote. In Houphouët-Boigny's Ivory Coast this was done with Stalinist efficiency: 98 per cent of the electorate voted, and 99.9 per cent of them voted against independence. In poor peripheral Guinea, where the chiefs had already been brought to heel, the resolve of Sekou Touré and his ruling party was enough to ensure a 95.2 per cent nationalist majority with 85.5 per cent voting. In Niger the governing party was also nationalist, but there was a major opposition party, and the chiefs

NOTES FOR PAGES 153 TO 156

were, crucially, against. See further F. Ansprenger, op. cit., chapter
17 and appendix.

51 'The era of nationalism has passed', the future President of Senegal
told a UNESCO audience in 1950, speaking as the representative
of France (F. Ansprenger, op cit., p. 166).

52 R. B. Collier, op. cit., p. 120.

53 Quoted from T. de Bary, *East Asian Civilizations*, Cambridge MA
1988, pp. 31f.

54 R. Ishii, *A History of Political Institutions in Japan*, Tokyo 1980,
pp. 104f and 98.

55 T. Ismael and J. Ismael, *Politics and Government in Islam*, New
York 1985.

56 B. Lewis, *The Political Language of Islam*, Chicago 1988, p. 1.

57 Sounding out lordly opinion had hardly been practised in Japan
for the two centuries preceding the emergence of Commodore
Perry in 1853, and there had been no representative city self-
government. The dynastic Ottoman Empire had dispensed with
classical Khalifa, principles of legitimacy, and also since the seventeenth century with any consultative institution (S. Mardin, *The
Genesis of Young Ottoman Thought*, Princeton 1962, p. 151). The
great Confucian tradition of China had conceptions of virtuous
and orderly rule, but did not provide any institutional controls
of the leader's rule. Nor, it seems, did any other of the Asian high
cultures: Bary, op. cit,; S. E. Finer, 'Notes towards a History of
Constitutions', in V. Bogdanor (ed.), *Constitutions in Democratic
Politics*, Aldershot 1988; J. Mabbett (ed.), *Patterns of Authority
and Kingship in Traditional Asia*, London 1985; B. Smith (ed.),
*Religion and Legitimation of Power in Thailand, Laos and Burma*,
Chambersburg PA 1978.

58 L. Dupree, *Afghanistan*, Princeton 1973, pp. 332f; V. Gregorian, *The Emergence of Modern Afghanistan*, Stanford CA 1969,
pp. 40f.

59 The corresponding Russian provincial *zemstvo* organization was
launched in 1864, and city councils in 1870.

60 My main Ottoman and Turkish teachers have been Mardin, op.
cit; R. Davison, 'The Advent of the Principle of Representation
in the Government of the Ottoman Empire', in W. Polk and R.
Chambers (eds), *Beginnings of Modernization in the Middle East*,
Chicago 1962; and E. Ösbudun, 'Turkey: Crises, Interruptions,
Reequilibrations', in L. Diamond, et al., op. cit., volume 3.

61 T. Vanhainen, *The Emergence of Democracy: A Comparative
Study of 119 States, 1850–1979*, Helsinki 1984, p. 142. It should
be added, perhaps, that in spite of the affirmation of representative politics by the nineteenth- and early twentieth-century Islamic

reform movement (Ismael and Ismael, op. cit., chapters 2–3), the most significant Muslim successor state to the Ottoman Empire, the Kingdom of Hijaz, since 1932 known as Saudi Arabia, went back on the Ottoman political reforms, allowing no elected legislature, and having a more officialist local administration than that of the Ottoman *ferman* of 1840. (The Hijaz Constitution and later changes may be found in the compilation by M. Khalil (ed.), *The Arab States and the Arab League: A Documentary Record*, vol. 1, Beirut 1962.)

62  Even if the shogunate had been abolished, no real power had been restored to the young emperor Meiji.

63  R. H. P. Mason, *Japan's First General Election, 1890*, Cambridge 1969.

64  R. H. P. Mason, op. cit., R. Ishii, op. cit.

65  R. H. P. Mason, op. cit., pp. 30 and 185.

66  Calculations from P. Flora, op. cit., vol. 1, chapter 3 and vol. 2, chapter 1.

67  In 1911 the Lower House had actually passed a wide suffrage bill. The Suffrage Bill of 1920 was parliamentarily outmanoeuvred, and the movement petered out.

68  See further P. Duus, *Party Rivalry and Political Change in Taisho Japan*, Cambridge MA 1968.

69  D. Pong and E. Fung (eds), *Ideal and Reality: Social and Political Change in Modern China, 1860–1949*, Lanham MD 1985; A. Nathan, *Chinese Democracy*, London 1986.

70  J. Fincher, *Chinese Democracy*, London 1981, p. 71.

71  J. Fincher, op. cit., p. 115 and D. Sternberger and B. Vogel, op. cit., p. 514, respectively.

72  They range from Iran and its Constitutionalist Revolution of 1906–9 and the Thai military modernizers of 1932 to the fully monarchical octroi of elections in Ethiopia in 1955 and in Afghanistan in 1964 – where an attempt in 1928 led to the king's fall, because it was associated with a proposal of monogamy and women's unveiling (Gregorian, op. cit., pp. 258ff) – and then, until 1990, the successfully stubborn royal absolutism of Nepal.

73  See the special issue of *Daedalus* (Winter 2000) devoted to Multiple Modernities.

# Index